# Frequency Meditation:

# An Alchemy of Mind

By Ellen Hartsfield

# Frequency Meditation:
# An Alchemy of Mind

WolfDancer Press

P.O. Box 4581

Durango, Colorado 81302


1st Edition

ISBN-13: 978-1517237370

ISBN-10: 1517237378

# Frequency Meditation: An Alchemy of Mind

Be sure that you have your doctor's full permission before beginning this or any other program that contains exercises or recommendations that make suggestions for health, well-being, or healing.

This author is not a medical professional or therapist of any kind. This author does not suggest or recommend the use of this or any technique for the treatment of physical, emotional, psychological, or personal problems of any kind without the approval of and while under the care of a physician, psychologist, and/or other appropriate health care providers.

It is the author's intent to present metaphysical ideas that readers may then choose or not choose to experiment with or investigate further. The author takes no responsibility of any kind for the readers' health or for their personal choices and actions.

—

# Acknowledgements

I would like to thank my husband, Larry, for his careful and insightful reading of this book. His suggestions made this work clearer and wiser. His editorial recommendations proved essential to the completion of this work and to its content.

# Dedication

This book is dedicated to my husband, Larry, my partner, colleague, fellow writer and editor, and above all else, my friend. Your love, kindness, and wisdom have enriched my life in ways beyond counting. Together, our books are better than they could have ever been if working alone, and our lives are far richer and more joyful and blessed than I could have ever imagined! Thank you.

After reviewing an early draft of this book, you used the ideas presented here to help you prepare and sit through a two and a half hour invasive dental procedure that involved drilling into the bone and working under the gums. Unlike the same procedure performed previously which was, by turns, horrible, painful, and rather terrifying, the second half of the procedure, on the other side of your mouth, and where the infection was much worse, went smoothly.

In fact, after reading this book, by the time you arrived at the dentist's office for round two of the procedure, you were relaxed, laughing, and in a great mood. You felt at peace throughout the entire procedure, cracked jokes, and afterwards recovered fully, quickly, and easily! Who knew that this meditation technique had a dental application?

You've since continued to experiment with the exercises and suggestions in this book and have continued to experience fantastic results in many areas of your life outside of a meditation practice. Amazing!

This book is also dedicated to the friends and coaching clients with whom I have reached states of deep meditative peace, stillness, and understanding. Together we have become weightless, rejoicing in knowing that we don't have any problems, that we never had any problems, that problems don't exist. Together we have touched the Peace of God.

# Table of Contents

The chapter headings in this book were given titles to honor different meditation techniques and traditions. The first portion of each chapter title gives the name of a meditation practice. The second part of each chapter title, the subheading, provides a clearer idea of the actual topic for that chapter.

# Monkey Mind: Introduction

I've developed the method of Frequency Meditation because I believe in the value of meditation and because I think that the common message from meditation teachers to "clear your mind" just isn't possible for most people.

Many students of meditation quickly become frustrated and do not have sufficient or effective practical tools to clear the mind aside from traditional directives such as to gaze at a candle flame, to count the in and out breaths, or to regard thoughts as clouds in the clear blue sky of one's true mind. The difficulty of clearing one's mind is recognized, of course, by all meditation traditions, but aside from calling this problem "monkey mind" or labeling it with another name, this problem isn't fully explained–at least not to my satisfaction.

The student is told, for example, to notice the clouds of thought, to understand that they're without substance and transitory, and to let them just flow by without engaging with them.

Why is this a problem? This method works if you stick with it long enough–you'll get there eventually; but why wait for "eventually?" The tools in this book are designed to help you skip eventually and get there now. Getting here now–and being here now–is the ultimate goal of all meditation.

# Clouds: An Alternative Method of Meditation

With the Frequency Meditation method I'll teach you to practice rising above the clouds in a step-by-step progression. Instead of wrestling with the clouds of thought or constantly trying to release them from the mind, you'll reach a higher cruising altitude–here we can imagine a jet flying at 35,000 feet–an atmospheric height that leaves the clouds far below. Not only is your mind now relaxing in its ideal vacation destination, unfettered by constant thinking, worry, and an itchy, twitchy body, but you've entered the jet stream, so to speak. You've got a tail wind that reduces drag and helps you speed forward, effortlessly, on your path.

The people to whom I've taught Frequency Meditation have been surprised at how quickly and easily they can move upwards into energy patterns that are naturally more silent, serene, and relaxing. They enter an elevated frequency and their mind and body begin to harmonize with this frequency, becoming more centered, calm, and peaceful.

This is a key concept. Different energy levels or frequencies each contain their own characteristics. Each frequency has a specific way that it behaves or feels. This idea will be explained in more depth a bit later on, but some frequencies that people typically inhabit contain a lot of nervous energy and some frequencies feel sad and depressed, whereas other frequencies are characterized by constant, restless thinking. When you enter that frequency's range, you begin to vibrate with that field, taking on its characteristics. With Frequency Meditation, you'll learn to consciously choose frequencies to use during meditation. Frequencies, or energetic mental and emotional states, exist in which there's little actual thinking going on, where the mind becomes quiet, and where the emotions are stilled. With Frequency Meditation you will learn how to work toward, recognize, and enter those serene, high-energy states of being.

As modern science has demonstrated again and again, everything is composed of energy and this energy moves at different rates. Photons, which are units of light, zoom by, not surprisingly, at the speed of light. Electrons, key building blocks of all matter, move around a central nucleus and can occupy spaces of lower energy or higher energy as they zip about.

In the world of electrons, a higher "orbit" moves faster than a lower one. Don't think about electrons moving along a prescribed path–exactly how they move is not understood, but the concept of an orbit is often employed in science and is a useful descriptor here. When an electron wants to vibrate at a higher frequency, it leaves its lower orbital trajectory and reappears at a higher one without first traversing the space in between the lower and the higher orbit. The electron simply reappears at the new frequency.

In frequency meditation, you're going to practice "jumping" into higher orbits, leaping from lower frequencies to more exalted ones without the need to slog your way, step by step, through the lower energy patterns. You'll start at your current frequency, which you'll learn how to measure, and then you'll leap up to a higher one. Then you'll leap up again.

The minimum jump you'll make by engaging in this form of meditation is a leap of a ten times higher increase in your energy field. With practice, you'll leap higher, faster, and with less effort. We're composed of innumerable electrons and we're going to practice behaving like them, leaping to higher orbits without ever needing to traverse the space in between.

Let's return for a moment to the imagery of our thoughts as clouds. During meditation those cloudy thoughts constitute stubborn, constant distractions and impediments in our mental landscape. These cloudy ideas are as substantial as vapor or air. Even though they're just mental clouds and lack density or solidity, they're surprisingly tenacious. The thoughts = clouds motif is an effective and beautiful image. Yet, with Frequency Meditation, rather than trying to make your thoughts go away, rather than working to release them, you select a target frequency and then let that frequency do the work for you.

You're not "quieting" your mind, you're learning to inhabit a realm in which the mind no longer reigns. You're gliding along at 35,000 feet, no longer able to even glimpse the clouds far below you. When you reach a high enough altitude through effective meditation, you'll discover that you're flying First Class–we all are–and that the ticket is free.

Again, there's nothing wrong with the idea of seeing thoughts as clouds that one doesn't want to try to hold onto any more than one would try to seize the cloud itself. Countless meditation students have been helped by this kind of imagery and related teachings. However, countless more prospective students of meditation have not been able to use the traditional teachings on how to release thoughts, on how not to get attached to them. Instead, sooner or later, the students become frustrated and either give up trying to meditate or treat meditation as an exercise in sitting quietly while constantly practicing the releasing of thought. That's helpful, but there's an easier and faster way to clear the mind of its frantic thought. Yes, Frequency Meditation still requires practice, but I believe that you'll begin to reach states of restful quiet, or even achieve the frequency realms of true silence, without needing to dedicate years of your life, or lifetimes, to its practice.

Of course, there are those who will not find the Frequency Meditation method any more helpful than other meditation methods, such as the meditation practices from the Buddhist traditions that have been around for a long time, or the more recent Transcendental Meditation that caught on in certain western circles in the hip 1960s. That's fine. At some point these meditation students will either overcome their resistance to rising above "the clouds" or another meditation technique will come along that will suit them perfectly.

Not only can the Frequency Meditation method assist many students of meditation to successfully meditate, perhaps for the first time, but it can also help practiced meditators move past thinking and words more successfully and enter into the silence that is our true home, fully inhabiting the serenity that resides within.

# The Candle: Dr. David Hawkins

To help you understand and practice Frequency Meditation, I first need to introduce some of the basic ideas behind the work of the late psychiatrist, Dr. David Hawkins, Ph.D. Dr. Hawkins had a thriving psychiatry practice in New York City yet suffered from numerous debilitating and life-threatening illnesses over a period of years. He spent approximately the last 30 years of his life in an awakened state in which all of his ailments, one by one, disappeared, and in which he felt deep peace and aliveness. He devoted much of that self-actualized time to writing, speaking, and teaching in order to help others shed the pain and confusion that accompanies most people in their walk through life, helping his students and readers gain greater clarity, serenity, and joy.

Dr. Hawkins created a scale from 1-1,000 which he used to calibrate the comparative energy levels of people, ideas, places, and events. When I began to read his books, I had several "aha" moments during which the various kinds of energy work I'd previously studied and the spiritual ideas I'd practiced came into greater focus and alignment with each other and within me. I began to combine his measurements of energy frequency with my daily spiritual practices and in my coaching work with clients. As I integrated his teachings with other spiritual practices, I then began to have many more "aha" moments. I created Frequency Meditation in response to a need that I saw in some of the people I worked with who had trouble meditating through more traditional means.

I found Dr. Hawkins' discussion of energetic frequency to be the clearest, most detailed, accurate, and helpful spiritual discussion of energy levels I have ever come across. As I studied his ideas, they began to integrate themselves into other teachings that I've studied and into information that has come to me on my own over the course of my deep meditation and intuitive listening. I started to see how Dr. Hawkins' work could be taught and used in new ways, honoring his contributions and achievements while continuing to develop his work for greater understanding, healing, and applicability. I began to combine his teachings with my own insights and, with some expansion and clarification, arranged the resulting spiritual practice into a specific, yet simple, methodology that could be used to help people meditate more effectively and to achieve greater mental clarity and peace of mind in their day-to-day lives.

This book and its meditation technique are the result of those insights.

# The Flame: The History and Usefulness of Muscle Testing

Before you begin to practice Frequency Meditation, it is essential to understand the basics of muscle testing, or applied kinesiology, as it is also known. Applied Kinesiology was developed in the 1960s by the chiropractor, Dr. George Goodheart, who, by the way, might have the best last name in the English language!

In the 1970s, John Diamond, M.D., another individual with a great last name, expanded the use of Applied Kinesiology as a means to test for a range of ideas and as a reliable physical conduit to the unconscious. Muscle testing, as Applied Kinesiology is more popularly known, continues to evolve, with researchers from a range of academic disciplines discovering new uses for this tool. It is easy to learn and has many helpful applications in daily life, the chief one being to test the truth, helpfulness, or validity of any idea or choice.

I use muscle testing in Frequency Meditation to calibrate the energetic level or personal frequency of my coaching clients before they start to meditate. Muscle testing is then used periodically during the meditation session as the practitioner of meditation continues to sit in silence until the desired frequency or mental state is achieved. Through muscle testing the meditators receive ongoing feedback about their current energetic state and can then modify their thinking and behavior in order to move themselves into higher energy patterns. These higher frequencies are naturally more serene, so it becomes easier for meditators to enter into stillness.

In the higher frequency states, words actually have difficulty appearing and organizing themselves in the mind. If one moves up a bit further, words are no longer present. The mind becomes completely quiet, effortlessly, and a deep peacefulness and sense of well-being infuses the meditator.

# Observing the Breath: Muscle Testing

In this section I describe a simple muscle testing technique that can be performed by one person without needing a partner to muscle test, as some of the methods require. I recommend that you use a computer to search for articles and images about muscle testing. You could use such search terms as "muscle testing made easy" or "muscle testing pictures and articles" as well as seek out videos online that demonstrate how to muscle test. To find helpful videos you might enter such search combinations as "YouTube O-ring muscle testing" or "videos with muscle testing explained."

If, like me, you learn best with a visual representation of what you're trying to learn, or if you are an auditory learner who needs to hear an explanation out loud, or if you're a kinesthetic learner who wants to immediately practice what you're trying to learn, a Google search for "O-ring muscle testing" should give you plenty of explanations and examples.

Here's my description of the technique. For some of you it might be enough to get started. Different forms of muscle testing exist, and the one I like most for Frequency Meditation involves making a circle with the thumb and index finger of one hand, then doing the same with the other hand so that the two circles are now linked together. You've just created a little infinity symbol or figure eight with your fingers. This formation is generally referred to as the "O-ring."

By using muscle testing, we can check to see whether a statement is true or false. We link two fingers from each hand together in these circles and then speak out loud or think in our minds a statement which we'd like to test. Even though you're seeking answers, don't phrase what you're testing as a question. Make a simple, direct statement such as, "Megan is the best person at work to select for my team." Then think or say the word "resist" while holding the two circles somewhat firmly and try to pull your hands apart. You don't want to hold the circles too tightly; you simply tell your mind to resist as you pull your fingers apart from each other in the linked ring formation.

Before working on the actual statements we wish to test for, it is a good idea to test out a couple of questions whose answers are clear and unambiguous in order to make sure that we're doing the muscle testing correctly and to make sure that we're over frequency 200, an idea that will be explained shortly. For example, try testing something obvious such as, "It is raining outside now." It is either raining right now where you are or it isn't, making this a clear and simple idea to test.

The idea behind muscle testing is that our bodies and minds know the truth of ideas even when our conscious minds do not. People always test weak (according to Dr. Hawkins' research on the subject), when they test to see if they should eat or drink food or beverages containing artificial sweeteners. Even if they love Diet Coke or sugar-free gum, they will immediately test "no" or "weak" for artificial sweeteners–it's a universal response because artificial sweeteners such as Splenda and Aspartame are universally harmful and dangerous to our health.

Try it now. Hold your hands in the O-ring intertwined circle position and state, "Artificial sweeteners are fine for me to eat" while thinking "resist" and try pulling your fingers apart. The two circles should come apart easily because artificial sweeteners contain neurotoxins, are extremely bad for our health and particularly for our brains and nervous systems, and this fact is true for anyone and everyone. Your fingers came apart, indicating a "weak" or "no" response.

On the other hand, if you wrote the word "love" on a piece of paper and then put it in a sealed envelope and tested different people to see whether or not they tested positively to the contents of the envelope while holding it, they should all test strong. A strong result is when the O-ring doesn't break easily, suggesting that your system is in positive alignment with the idea for which you're testing. In short, if your fingers successfully resist the statement, that is considered to be a "strong" or a "yes" response, but when your fingers come apart easily, you've just received a "no" response.

You could try this experiment for yourself, putting the name "Hitler" in one envelope (one of the experiments used by Dr. Hawkins) and "angels," for example, in another. Even a Nazi sympathizer who doesn't know what's in the envelope should test negative for Hitler. Hitler was bad for people's health. He and the atrocities he committed vibrate at an incredibly low frequency. Our systems intuitively know that the contents of the Hitler envelope are noxious and destructive. Our systems automatically and intuitively declare a very loud "no" in response to the concept of Hitler by having our fingers immediately unlink.

People holding the "angel" envelope should test positive when they don't know what's in the envelope, even if they don't believe in angels and even if they are atheists. Angels are a heavenly, beatific concept and people will test positively to something that expresses the feelings of love, kindness, and support.

Before muscle testing for my frequency level or for questions to which I want to know the answer, I like to first do a quick test to make sure that I'm in a proper frame of mind to do this work. I begin by stating my name. I want to make sure that I'm going to receive accurate, reliable responses through muscle testing.

Holding my hands in the two circles position, I then "resist" while stating my name. You can check your readiness to do a series of muscle tests by saying, "My name is Nancy." If this is a true statement for you, your fingers should hold strong, indicating a response of "true." Obviously, you should use your own name when testing for truth.

Next try saying that your name is something that it isn't. For example, I can then say, "My name is Herbert" and try to pull the rings apart while maintaining a bit of resistance. My encircled fingers should come apart right away.

I like to do another test to make sure that I'm getting an accurate response before I go on to the questions I actually want to check. I usually say, "Today is Monday" or whatever day of the week it actually happens to be. Again, this statement should test positive. The fact that today is Monday is either objectively true or it isn't–it's not a matter of opinion. Accepted facts are a good way to make sure that you're receiving a positive result for something that is true and a negative one in response to a false statement.

If you're having trouble getting an accurate reading when you test for a factual statement to which you know the answer (I am _____ years old. I live in the United States. I like fried chicken. I have a brother, and so on), keep practicing. Like any other skill, you'll get better and better at accurately muscle testing by regularly practicing this technique. After a while it will become second nature. At this point I rarely encircle my fingers when I muscle test. Instead, "yes" or "no" simply appears as soon as the question forms in my mind; I feel or hear the answer immediately and leave out all the steps that I used to do while I was still developing my skill at muscle testing.

You can test whether or not it would be better for your system to have carrots or peas for dinner. "It is best for my health for me to have carrots with dinner." "It is best for my health for me to have peas with dinner." "In terms of my health, it doesn't matter whether I have carrots or peas with dinner." "It is best for my health for me to have both carrots and peas with dinner."

You can test whether or not you should trust what someone is telling you. "John is telling me the truth when he says _____." "John believes that he is telling me the truth when he says _____." "What John is saying is false."

You can test for the integrity of a political candidate. "Candidate X is running for office in order to make money." "Candidate X is running for office for personal gain." "Candidate X is self-absorbed." "Candidate X usually tells the truth." "Candidate X often tells lies." Candidate X is a narcissist." "Candidate X has the well-being of all of his constituents in mind each time he votes on a bill." "Candidate X is a sociopath." "Candidate X is a psychopath." "Candidate X will help to make this country a better place." "Candidate X will make decisions that will harm this country and its people." "Candidate X is usually above frequency 200." "Above 250." "Above 300." "Above 350." "Above 400." Ideally, all of our leaders, whether in business, politics, medicine, or any other field that directly impacts the public good and safety would regularly test above 410, with registering at 450 or in the high 400s or low 500s being truly ideal. Again, what these numbers mean and how to use them when you meditate will be explained shortly.

Notice how each question is tested for individually, not as a compound sentence or as a sentence with multiple parts. You also never want to have questions embedded within questions. If you made the statement, "Candidate X trades votes for gifts from lobbyists and has connections to arms dealers" and then received a "no" answer, does that mean that the candidate doesn't do either? Does the "no" instead refer to one of the statements and not to the other? Good muscle testing uses short, simple, unambiguous statements.

# Mindfulness: Understanding Frequency 200

Becoming skilled at muscle testing is important and takes practice. At the same time, a key reason why one can receive an inaccurate answer to a muscle test, or a false negative or a false positive answer, is because one is under frequency 200, even if temporarily, on Dr. Hawkins' scale.

What does a frequency of 200 on the Hawkins scale mean? I'll go into the entire scale in more detail shortly, but if someone is above 200, that person's thinking has begun to move in a positive direction. When people are above 200 on this energetic scale, their choices are healthier the further above 200 they go. Above frequency 200, their thoughts and decisions increasingly support both their personal growth and the greater good.

Conversely, below 200 a person's thinking is increasingly negative, low energy, and destructive. When trying to muscle test while having a personal frequency under 200, the answers one receives in response to muscle testing will be inaccurate. The lower the frequency, the more negative and oppositional that person will be. Each point one moves down the scale represent a ten-fold decrease in energy levels. Therefore, having a frequency of 175 is a much lower and more negative energy state than having one at 195, which, although still negative, is getting closer to the break-even point of 200.

Clearly, we are all healthiest and happiest when we're over 200 on the Hawkins scale. For example, a person at 250 is much more positive, helpful, and hard-working than someone at 215, and she's enormously more positive and happy than someone at 180.

All of us give to the world, at least somewhat. We may hold the door open for another person, give a friend a ride even if it's a bit out of our way, help others carry their groceries, pick up some trash we see lying on the ground, and so on. We all receive from the world as well. I didn't grow my own food, grow the cotton to make the clothes I'm wearing, let alone dye and weave the fabric and sew the garments. We give and receive all of the time. However, a person under 200 takes more from the world and others than she gives in return. The further below frequency 200 a person is, the more she takes.

200 is the break-even point, possessing a kind of balance in which the positive thinking and the negative thinking of the individual are in equal proportions and in which giving and receiving are even. As a person moves above the critical 200 point, she begins to give more and more as compared to how much she takes or receives. She becomes increasingly helpful and encouraging. As she rises higher on the scale she will actually seek out ways to be of service.

Some people take a lot from others and from society as a whole. Social security and unemployment benefits are examples of something to which most people who work contribute and then, if they're unemployed for a time or when they retire, they can then draw from these resources. They give, and then they may receive in return.

Long-term welfare, on the other hand, is not a successful system because it often leads to keeping people, families, and even communities stuck at a low frequency in which they're dependent on others for many of their basic needs. Instead, "workfare" requires that people increase their levels of education, learn new job skills, or work in order to receive benefits. Working, learning, studying, and contributing to the larger society all help to raise a person's energy frequency, thereby making it more and more possible for them to take good care of themselves and, as they continue to move up the energy continuum, not only to require less external support but also to begin to contribute more in various ways to their communities and to the people around them.

In order to attain and maintain a high energetic frequency, it is important to develop the habit of giving. Giving might not have anything to do with money at all. The giving could involve listening better to friends and family, helping out more around the home, being friendlier to neighbors and colleagues, volunteering at a soup kitchen, or helping out in the community by filling and placing sand bags if a river is threatening to flood.

We cannot maintain high frequencies, even if we were once at a high energy level, unless we are giving to others, whether via our time, our talents, our prayers, or our personal resources. This is why if a person who retires wants to maintain good health (good health and a higher frequency tend to go hand in hand), he or she must continue to be involved in the larger world and find ways to contribute in life and to the world. They can volunteer in hospitals or museums, tutor in schools, support the arts in the towns where they live, join charitable organizations, and otherwise find ways to use their time and resources for the betterment of others. One person I know who at this stage in life is largely confined to bed is currently working to improve the English and literacy of his caregiver. This action is a great example of how, when one is willing, there is always a way to contribute to others, to make a difference, and to know that one's life matters. People who find ways to give to others feel better and are healthier. They are happier human beings and they're propelling themselves forward on their life path.

In short, contributing to others and to society raises people's energy frequency. Raising their energy frequency increases the amount of energy and the quality of energy they have with which to live their lives. Raising their frequency makes them, inevitably, want to be helpful and to find ways to contribute to others, which makes them feel better because it raises their energy. It's a happy cycle, not a vicious one.

Another key way to raise one's energy frequency is by continuing to learn, acquiring information and developing new skills while further expanding old ones. When we're learning, we're growing. When we're growing, we're healing. If we're healing, we're increasing our energetic frequency, which helps us to heal and grow. It's a happy cycle.

Level 200 in the Hawkins scale is the point at which a negative engagement with thinking, with other people, and with life itself begins to turn around and become more positive, giving, nurturing, helpful, and loving, step by step, as one progresses up the frequency ladder.

Meditation under 200 doesn't work. It is an exercise in frustration and futility, and the lower along the scale one is, the more difficult it is to center the mind. Under 200, the personal mind, or ego, is in charge of the individual. The personal mind, the egoic self, is competitive, restless, vain, antagonistic, and self-absorbed. When led by the ego, the mind doesn't consistently want to be still, it doesn't want to be peaceful, and it certainly doesn't want to find the spiritual home of God within. Instead, the egoic mind flits from one idea to the next, from one goal to another, agitated and distracted.

By raising one's frequency, one begins the process of leaving the ego behind. We don't fight with the ego. The ego has lots of practice with argument, struggle, and war and will win almost any engagement. Instead, as we clear and raise our frequency we begin to forget about egoic preoccupations and concerns as we set our mind and our sights on higher, gentler goals.

Starting at 200 there is a glimmer of light, of hope, as the individual slowly begins to take charge of himself, of his mood, of his choices, and of his thinking.

When we remember that under 200 one is in a fundamentally negative and oppositional state and above 200 one begins to think in healthier, more life-affirming and supporting ways, which would you rather marry? Someone under 200 or over 200? Which would you rather hire? Someone under 200 or over 200? Which would you rather elect to Congress? Someone under 200 or over 200? Which would you rather have as a friend? Someone under 200 or over 200? Which would you rather have as a boss? Someone under 200 or over 200? Which would you rather have your son or daughter date? Someone under 200 or over 200?

People over frequency 200 are happier, more peaceful, kinder, and more productive in helpful, positive ways. People over frequency 200 are participating in the gradual healing of the world, its environment, institutions, and attitudes. People over frequency 200 are helping to reduce the likelihood of war, are better neighbors, both locally and internationally, and are a lot more fun to be around.

Which one would you rather be? It's your choice in every situation, in all of your relationships, and in each moment of your life.

# I Am: Overcoming Frequency 200

When I test for it right now, I get that about 76% of the people on the planet resonate under frequency 200 at the moment of this writing. I also calibrate that approximately 48% of people living in the United States right now test under 200. 76 is about 63% more than 48. That's a lot. That's really significant.

A bit more than half of the population in the United States tends to register above frequency 200 at any given moment. Unfortunately, that is not yet close to true for many parts of the world, and the results of that lower frequency range is readily apparent in the daily lives of those souls.

If you think about it, without even having patriotism enter into the equation at all, it is logical that the people living in the United States would, on average, rate in the positive rather than in the negative range. Why does this make sense? Because most Americans have a roof over their heads and walls around them, and those walls are generally not made of cardboard. Most Americans have access to clean running water, electricity, and indoor plumbing. Most Americans go to school when they're young, schooling which is free below the college level. And so on.

I'm not saying that the United States is somehow perfect. Everyone of us could make a list in this moment of the many ways in which this country, from the local to the national levels, could be a stronger, healthier, fairer, more respectful, and a greater country that took better care of all of its citizens. We still have plenty of work to do.

Other countries where much of the populace enjoys relative peace and safety, access to a good free education and a standard of living that covers most daily necessities, the availability of quality healthcare, and other markers of developed society, also tend to have a similar percentage of the population that registers over frequency 200 at any given moment. More countries around the world are joining the "high frequency club" all of the time as they improve their infrastructure, educational and health care systems, and clean up and protect their environments.

The frequency levels recently have been steadily and gradually increasing in the United States and in other countries that are governed by a philosophy of protecting and uplifting its citizens. Over the last decades or centuries, depending upon where we are talking about, more and more people around the world are enjoying a cleaner, safer, healthier daily life and a higher standard of living.

The United States could never have become a world leader as long as it continued to practice slavery. The United States could never have become the powerhouse that it continues to be without working on developing a fairer and more tolerant legal system, expanding its educated work force, creating planned cities and towns that include public transportation and opportunities for recreation, and developing its industry and technology. The United States could not successfully participate in a global vision for the world's future without its state and national parks, without its excellent colleges and universities, and without the many creative people working in TV, movies, music, comedy, and other creative arts. In fact, if we truly understood how energy frequencies work at both the personal and national levels, art and music would become the last classes we would cut during a budget crisis, not the first!

In other words, if a country wants to increase its overall frequency, thereby increasing its global standing, strength, and economic position, it needs to invest more of its resources, proportionately, in quality education, the arts and sciences, technology, human rights, caring for the environment, and healthy opportunities for leisure and relaxation, such as bike paths, protected forests, and public beaches.

# Heart: Our Ever-changing Frequencies

Our energy frequencies are not static. We all fluctuate in our energy levels throughout the day and from day to day. If we're angry, frustrated, impatient, rude, sad, or frightened, in that moment we will register under 200 even if shortly beforehand we were at 250, 280, or even higher. We were at a higher frequency until we were triggered by our own thoughts or by the thoughts and emotions we selected, however unconsciously, in response to some external event. We could be at 240 and then hear a discussion of 9-11 on the TV, complete with images of the destruction of the twin towers, and it is likely that we will suddenly find ourselves plummeting under frequency 200.

On the other hand, if we're at 260, for example, and then put on some beautiful music and dance around the kitchen a bit as we do the dishes, pausing once in a while to enjoy in the trees outside the window and to give thanks for the food we just ate that made the washing of dishes necessary, we might jump up to 310, 350, or even into the 400s.

Fluctuating energy frequencies are the norm. When we think positive thoughts, we will engage in more positive actions and we'll move upwards in our energy frequency. When we think negative thoughts, we will engage in more negative behaviors such as arguing and complaining, and our energy signature will be much lower. We have all endlessly jumped around the energy frequency spectrum and we will all do so many, many more times, but now we can begin to work with our energy in a much more conscious, deliberate way, actively creating the moods, the experiences, and the life we want.

If we're feeling happy, optimistic, enthusiastic, calm, relaxed, or if we're laughing (but not if we're using laughter to mock or deride other people), then we are over 200. Using humor to hurt people's feelings and to increase our own standing or that of our "in-group" at the expense of another person or "out-group" derives from thinking and decisions made under frequency 200.

On the other hand, using humor to make fun of people or situations by such comics as John Stewart during his show filled with political humor or Wayne Brady on a game show that he hosts are an exception to idea of dropping under 200 due to mocking humor. The humor in these cases is more well-intentioned, used to help people see their foibles in gentle ways, or to awaken, to teach, and to point out injustice and dishonesty. These are examples of elevated frequency individuals and of a high use of humor. Wayne Brady's teasing is light-hearted and creates a sense of "in-group," using humor the way close friends do, giving each other silly nicknames or poking fun. The satire that a political humorist such as John Stewart engages in has a moral purpose and is designed to point out the gap between our unexamined thoughts and reality; the reduction in this gap can make us more aware, informed, ethical, and conscious.

# Names of God: The Hawkins Scale

Dr. Hawkins' scale ranges from 0-1,000 and is a logarithmic scale like the Richter scale that is used to measure the magnitude of earthquakes. In Dr. Hawkins' scale, each time we move up one number on the scale, that number's power is then multiplied by ten, creating an enormous increase in energy from the previous digit on the scale. In other words, on the Hawkins scale, the number two is actually ten times higher than the number one. The number three is ten times higher than two and 100 times higher than one; we're multiplying an increasing number by ten each time we move up a point on the scale.

The number four is ten times higher than three and 1,000 times higher than one. By the time you reach the number seven, the value of seven is one million times higher than the number one. A shift of six points results in about one million times more energy! It isn't necessary to understand exactly how logarithmic scales work; it is enough to understand that on this scale, with each increase of one point higher, you've multiplied the preceding number by 10. You can see that by moving up just a few points on the scale one moves up thousands, millions, or billions of times higher, and so on. If the scale were plotted as a graph, the line would point steeply upwards from its starting point.

If one person registers at frequency 215 in a given moment and another person registers at 225, the difference in energetic frequency between them is actually quite huge, but it's still nothing when compared to two people, or two nations, having a conversation when one of them is at 215 and the other is at 320. Energetic discrepancies like this happen all of the time and can lead to tremendous misunderstandings between individuals or groups. Since my energy frequency generally tends to range between 450-610 at this point in my life, when I'm teaching and the average range of the students in the room is about 230, or when I'm talking to a friend registering at about 275, I might consciously lower my energy frequency somewhat for a while just to improve communication between us.

At the same time that I'm lowering my energy a bit, the people I'm talking to are unconsciously raising their energy levels. This happens naturally because most people tend to mirror the people around them, picking up their turns of phrase, their stance, and their mannerisms while talking to them. In the same way, we automatically tend to vibrate at least a bit closer to the people we're near.

Your mother was right when she told you that she didn't want you to hang out with certain people. The choices we make about where, how, and with whom we spend our time are essential in shaping our energy signatures at that moment and over time, a pattern that directly influences the trajectory and quality of our lives.

Have you ever noticed that after you spend some time with a particular friend you often discover afterwards that you're feeling dejected, depressed, or moody, but earlier in the day you'd been feeling great? Chances are that they tend to have a lower "set point," than you do.

The "set point" is my term for the unconscious frequency at which we tend to vibrate naturally. You've probably noticed that spending time with some people gives you a lift and that you laugh more together. You feel encouraged, supported, and just generally happier. Those individuals likely have a similar or higher set point as compared to you or happen to be resonating at a higher frequency than you are at that moment.

By learning Frequency Meditation you will learn how to gauge your frequency levels, the frequency levels of places and situations around you, and those of other people. You will also begin to increase your set point so that you start to vibrate at a higher and higher frequency.

Raising the set point at which you generally vibrate will make you happier. Raising your set point will make your relationships smoother and easier. Learning to increase your energetic frequency, even by a few points, will help your children live more happily in the world. Remember that the people around us are always influenced by our frequency levels, just as we're affected by theirs, whether we know it consciously or not. You'll be more productive and effective at work as your set point increases. At the same time, as you improve your energy levels you'll be making a greater contribution to the healing of the world, point by point, bit by bit.

Your frequency shapes your mood, the quality of your thinking, and your worldview. I'm going to teach you how to begin to check your frequency level and how to raise it, even if at first you're only able to raise it up for a brief while, and even if you're only able to raise it up by just a couple of points. As we are beginning to see, raising your frequency level up even by a few points can result in a huge improvement in your emotional well-being, effectiveness, clarity of thought, and even health.

In the Hawkins scale, people cannot go lower than 0, even if they are extremely negative, and they cannot go above 1,000, no matter how kind, helpful, and wise they become. This scale from 0-1,000 describes the complete range that people can occupy, energetically, during their lifetimes on earth. The range over 1,000 constitutes higher frequencies than those that are possible for people living on our planet. For example, the frequencies inhabited by beings from the angelic realms are much higher than anything that people can strive for on earth; during an earthly lifetime, 1,000 is as high as it gets, and getting to that frequency is incredibly rare.

# Counting the Breath: Specific Measurements on The Hawkins Scale

Dr. Hawkins provided the following descriptors of some of the energy frequencies on his scale and the mental states and attitudes that are characteristic of each level:

| | | |
|---|---|---|
| 0 | - | death |
| 20 | - | shame |
| 30 | - | guilt |
| 50 | - | apathy |
| 75 | - | grief |
| 100 | - | fear |
| 125 | - | desire |
| 150 | - | anger |
| 175 | - | pride |
| 200 | - | courage |
| 250 | - | neutrality |

| 310 | - | willingness |
| 350 | - | acceptance |
| 400 | - | reason |
| 500 | - | love |
| 540 | - | joy |
| 600 | - | peace |
| 700-1,000 | - | enlightenment |

(From *Power vs. Force: The Hidden Determinants of Human Behavior*, 2013 edition, pages 90-91.)

With a frequency under 200, people have a reversed polarity. A reversed polarity means that their energy is cycling in an opposite direction to that of health, truth, and well-being. People who are under frequency 200 are drawn to negative, false, and harmful ideas and actions and push away or are suspicious of helpful people, concepts, and choices.

In the method of energy work called Energy Balancing, when people's thinking is negative and their choices are counterproductive, they're considered to be in an energetic stated referred to as a "spin inversion." When I began to read Dr. Hawkins' work, I realized that what Energy Balancing calls a "spin inversion," or a state of reversed polarity, could only occur if an individual was cycling under frequency 200 on the Hawkins scale.

In the tapping method of EFT, used to heal and release phobias, trauma, anxiety, and other issues that impede health and well-being, when a person has conscious or unconscious thoughts and beliefs that are counterproductive and that impede their health and growth, that point of view is labeled "objections." Again, as I studied Dr. Hawkins' writings, I realized that this reversed energetic state named "objections" in the energy psychology treatment modality known as EFT (Emotional Freedom Technique) referred to an energetic blockage their system that was resonating under frequency 200 on the Hawkins scale.

What we label the resistant state doesn't really matter, but the state of having a reversed polarity or of being against an idea, an event, or the moment itself, and therefore of being under frequency 200 around a particular issue, means that you're in a state of resistance or opposition at that time. Aside from being angry, anxious, depressed, or frustrated, it is clear that one cannot be a successful meditator when one is opposed to the moment in which one finds oneself. It is essential to be able to recognize oppositional states right away in oneself so that one can immediately work to correct them.

The farther below the break-even frequency of 200 a person is at a given moment, the more deeply he or she will be entrenched in a state of reversed polarity. Bad choices will attract them. Taking drugs, encouraging other people to drink and/or take drugs, unsafe driving, including while under the influence of a mind-altering substance, hitting children in order to teach them a lesson, speaking rudely and unkindly to other people, not taking responsibility for oneself and one's life, and other sorts of destructive or reckless behavior will make sense to them, will actually appeal to them, and they'll easily be able to justify thinking, speaking, and acting in hostile, fearful, unhelpful, or dangerous and irresponsible ways.

If people register under 200 for more than a just a little while or if they are quite a bit under 200 (say at 190 or lower), they will be drawn to negative attractors such as artificial sweeteners (to which, as mentioned earlier, everyone tests negatively), poor choices, and selfish, hostile political beliefs and agendas. They'll be repelled by or disinterested in positive attractors such as equal rights for all citizens. To state the obvious, a belief in the intrinsic equality of your fellow human beings is a sign of an elevated frequency level. Judging or hating people who don't respect or favor equality for all groups of people registers at a low frequency, just as does the discriminatory behavior itself.

In order to function happily and well in life, it is necessary to spend most of one's time above 200. Spending all of one's time above energy frequency 200 would be ideal, but people, at least periodically, get angry, impatient, sad, or scared, and they sometimes blame, shame, and inflict guilt on other people, or try to manipulate through guilt or threat. Energy frequencies, what they mean personally and in the larger world and how to work with them effectively, are discussed in much greater depth in my book, *The Alchemy of Change*.

So what, more specifically, are these energy frequencies that I'm talking about? In the scale that Dr. Hawkins developed to measure the energy levels of people, the lowest number is 0, which is death, the state of not having an organized and functioning energetic system operating in one's body.

One thousand is the highest level that a person can attain and still maintain a coherent physical body. 1,000 represents perfect enlightenment in terms of the thinking and experiences of this earth. Profound spiritual awareness and peace exist in the range of 700-1,000. In my experience, unless people want to join an ashram or a monastery or otherwise dedicate the entirety of their lives to God, people should only raise up their energy during meditation to a maximum, say, of around 720 or 730, and even then not for very long. Of course, most people have never experienced those states in their lifetime and don't know how to enter them. Moving your energy up into the low 700s for brief periods of meditation is exactly what this book aims to teach you. At 700 the mind is completely still and at peace, effortlessly, and you're infused with a sense of calm beingness.

Attempting to clear one's mind is an absolutely futile task for most people because most people do not know how to raise their energy into the 500s or higher. In fact, many people spend much of their time a bit below or above 200, and the mind is frantic and disorganized in that frequency range.

As one enters the 300s, one's thinking becomes clearer and more organized. It becomes much easier to focus and to hold an idea in one's mind for a longer period of time. One feels generally calmer and has an easier time sitting still and listening, both within and without.

As one enters the 400s, one's thinking is more centered and peaceful. There is less noise in the mind and periodically small gaps in thinking and in the flow of words through consciousness begin to appear.

Beginning in the 500s, the start of the spiritual realm, the mind has more space and openness and can maintain periods of calm and quiet which rejuvenate the body and bring peace to one's thoughts and senses.

# Contemplation: Preparing for Frequency Meditation

Before beginning this meditation practice, you first need to learn how to muscle test. Once you feel that you have a pretty good idea how muscle testing works and have become fairly proficient at it, then start to check your energetic frequency level on the Hawkins scale. I recommend that you do this for about a week, consistently, at least three times a day, perhaps in the morning, around noon, and again at night. You want to get a sense of your old energetic comfort zones. Knowing where you started will help you to genuinely appreciate the gains you make, not just during the times when you practice Frequency Meditation, but in your daily life as well.

How do you muscle test to check your frequency? While using your O-ring hand formation and while thinking "resist" say, "I am now at frequency 200 or above." Then check for a strong (your fingers hold) or a weak (your fingers slide apart easily) response. If you don't receive a positive response at 200, you need to do some of the exercises listed in this book to help you to improve your energetic frequency. Be sure to do what you can to keep your frequency over 200, that is, in the positive, healthy, helpful range, whether you're sitting down to meditate or not.

Next say, "I am now at frequency 210 or above." Continue with, "I am now at frequency 220 or above." If you feel that you're much higher than this, check your level by counting by 50's. "I'm now at frequency 300 or above." "I'm now at frequency 350 or above." And so on. When you get a weak response to a level that you're checking, back up to get more specific information. If your system went weak when you tested for "250 or above," now try, "I'm now at frequency 240 or above." If that's weak, back up your testing by another 10 points and check again. If you received a strong, positive response at 240, but not at 250, now check for each point in between. Say, "I'm now at frequency 241 or above." Then try, "I'm now at frequency 242 or above." Test until you know your specific frequency. Note it down in a journal or log. Again, it's helpful to know your starting point before you begin a meditation session in order to observe how meditation impacts your frequency level and so that you can observe your energy shifting and recalibrating over time.

Meanwhile, of course, you can meditate using your old methods while getting ready to use this one. True success with Frequency Meditation usually requires some understanding of Hawkins' scale and your own frequency tendencies, so I suggest that you take a week to practice muscle testing and to familiarize yourself with the ideas in this book. Then you'll be ready to work with Frequency Meditation in your daily life.

In what range do you spend most of your time? Are there times of day when you typically go higher or lower? When? Are there situations or places that bring you up or down? Be specific. Does spending time around certain people send you into a tailspin? Do you notice any triggers, words, sounds, tastes, and so on, that tend to propel you lower? Really start paying attention to your frequency numbers and record them on your phone or computer or in an old-fashioned paper journal. This information will be helpful to you as you proceed.

# Om: How to Practice Frequency Meditation

Before you start to meditate, first use muscle testing to check your frequency level. If you're below 200, you won't be able to meditate no matter which method you use, so you must first raise your energy level. Even if you're below about frequency 310, you will still have a tremendously difficult time stilling your thoughts, calming your body, and sitting in peace. You can try to meditate at frequency 210, 275, or 300, for example, but I recommend that when you're ready to practice Frequency Meditation you first check your starting frequency, then drink some water with lemon or lime juice so that you're hydrated and your body is more alkaline, and next work on increasing your frequency. Once you've done a couple of exercises to increase your energy level, test yourself again and then sit down quietly to begin.

With practice it will become easier and easier to raise your energy level. You will also begin to notice, to really feel, when your energy level is dropping or low. In that case you can immediately work to improve your energy level. By observing yourself at various frequencies, you'll learn what each frequency feels and looks like. You'll notice the kinds of thoughts that you think at different levels. At 150, you're going to think angry thoughts. At 100, you're going to be absorbed by fearful thoughts. At 125 you're going to fantasize about having sex or about getting a lot of money and about buying things. At 310 you'll think about completing tasks on your internal to-do list and you'll probably have the energy and focus to get started on them right away.

Those are some of the general patterns that people will experience. You want to notice the broader and universal patterns such as those of grief or guilt, and you also want to pay attention to some of the more specific and personal trends that make up your own thinking at different frequencies. If you like, quickly jot down, in a very few words, the patterns that you observe in yourself at various levels. You don't want to get stuck in a long conversation with yourself about your "problems" or get drawn into the stories that you tell yourself. Engaging with the problem can quickly become a distraction and take you off your path. Notice, make a quick note if you like, and then immediately return to choosing a frequency and a set of thoughts that nurture, heal, and support the good in your life.

With time and practice you'll also be able to maintain a higher frequency for longer periods of time. This practice of holding a higher frequency level will improve your life in terms of the quality of your relationships, your degree of inner peace, your mood, your finances, and in many other ways.

If you decide that you want to increase your energy frequency before beginning to meditate, or just because it's a great thing to do, I'm including a list of useful strategies to help you raise your energy frequency.

# Guided Imagery: Techniques for Increasing Your Frequency

- Put on some inspiring, beautiful music.

- Get up a dance around for a bit.

- Get some exercise.

- Listen to an inspiring TED talk, audiobook, or Podcast.

- Watch an inspiring YouTube video.

- Read a few pages or a chapter of an inspirational, upbeat, wise book, article, or Blog.

- Play a musical instrument, even if you don't play it well.

- Sing, even if you don't sing well.

- Tell some jokes.

- Do some yoga, Tai Chi, or Qi Gong.

- Take some slow, deep, relaxing breaths.

- Do some stretching exercises.

- Hum, and on the exhale say "Ahhhhh" while holding a tone or note.

- Say "om" a few times while breathing out and holding a tone. Make sure that you take your time saying the "o" in this little word.

- Draw.

- Paint.

- Sculpt.

- Knit, sew, or crochet.

- Write a poem.

- Do crafts that you enjoy.

- Read some poems, especially ones that bring you a sense of peace or joy.

- Learn a few new words or expressions in another language.

- Engage in the arts.

- Send a card, email, or text with a positive message to another person.

- Watch laughing baby videos on the Internet.

- Watch cute, happy animal videos on the Internet.

- Give attention to, care for, and play with your pet.

- Watch TV or instructional videos in order to learn something new or in order to develop a skill you currently possess.

- Watch inspiring, wise, or funny TV, videos, or movies. Don't watch horror movies, movies that involve scary supernatural topics (such as shows with vampires), or ones that involve negative sexual practices that frighten, subjugate, harm, or threaten to harm the participants.

- Do some laughter yoga.

- Select a natural scent such as lavender, orange, peppermint, lemongrass, or tea tree oil (not one of those artificial scented sprays or candles that you find in most supermarkets–in this case it's worth it to spend a bit more and have a quality product that is organic and was developed from essential oils, not chemicals) and put a few drops in a diffuser or in a scent dispenser.

- State some positive affirmations such as "I completely love and accept myself" or "I feel free and at ease" or "My life is a gift" or "I choose joy."

- Look at nature.

- Take a short walk in nature.

- Look at pictures online of beautiful scenery such as tropical beaches, flowers, birds, waterfalls, snowy landscapes, mountains, or forests.

- Light some dried sage (Many stores sell little bundles of sage for burning, carefully, of course. It's also easy to grow and dry your own.) and use it to clear and bless the energy in your home.

- Hold a crystal in your hand and feel its healing energy infuse your body.


- Smile.


- Smile while holding an image in your mind of someone you love.


- Smile and give thanks for this moment.


- Hold a crystal in your hands and visualize it clearing you of all negativity. If you don't have a crystal or if you want to try this exercise differently, look up images of crystals online (a search for "images of healing crystals" or "images of citrine" or "images of malachite" or "images of rose quartz," etc.) and gaze at an image or images of crystals while releasing any negativity you encounter within your body-mind. Send the negativity outwards and upwards, out of your room or home and into the heavens. Imagine all resistance just floating out of your body as the crystal clears your system. Visualize the resistance or negativity completely dissolving as it moves far away from you.

- Stand barefoot on the floor or outside and gently bounce your knees up and down. With each exhale relax and say, "ha, ha, ha" and imagine tension flowing out of your body.

- Stand barefoot on the floor or outside, make sure that your knees are not locked, and breathe down into the earth with each exhale and draw healing energy up into your body with each inhale.

- Give thanks for your life.

- Express gratitude to another person.

- Express gratitude to God.

- Express gratitude to yourself for wanting to heal and grow.

- Give yourself credit for three helpful, thoughtful things you've done recently.

- Do something thoughtful for another person such as sending a kind note to them or making little homemade gifts to give out for the holidays.

- Give yourself credit for a time when you demonstrated great courage in the face of hardship or loss.

- Think three kind thoughts about a friend.

- Think four kind thoughts about someone you don't like.

- Say a prayer for a friend.

- Say a prayer for a family member.

- Say a prayer for a colleague.

- Say a prayer for a neighbor.

- Say a prayer for the honor and wisdom of your government.

- Say a prayer for your country.

- Say a prayer for another country.

- Say a prayer for someone you don't like.

- Give thanks for anything and everything you can think of.

Some of these activities will take quite a while. They're intended to help you learn how to raise your energy frequency overall. Painting a picture or taking a hike while admiring the beauty around you are worthwhile activities in and of themselves and will align your energetic state with higher energies. With time you will begin to naturally vibrate a bit higher and then a bit higher again.

Other activities listed here are quick fixes to your energy state. Each one of them, if done effectively, should raise your energy signature by at least a few points. If you need to raise your energy level up a bit higher before beginning to meditate, do your favorite exercise a few times. You could also mix and match, practicing a few of these exercises before checking your frequency again. Depending upon what you select and what your starting frequency is, you should be ready to meditate fairly quickly.

Some of these activities will raise your frequency higher than others. Taking a walk might raise your frequency to 250 or 275. Taking a walk while listening to beautiful music might easily raise your frequency to 410 or higher. Taking that same walk while listening to an inspiring book or, for example, an audio recording of a lecture by Eckhart Tolle or Dr. Hawkins, can take your frequency even higher.

If you're walking or hiking in a beautiful place, somewhere where you can admire birds, flowers, or other natural beauty, your energy field will naturally be uplifted. That walk, taken with a friend who agrees to find topics to talk about that are positive, will help to support a strong frequency. Remember that joining two or more in prayer or in the effort to heal, bless, and grow greatly increases the potency of what you're doing.

Gardening is another positive means of enjoying and contributing to natural beauty and your health while improving your energy level.

Fishing and hunting, when practiced ethically and carefully and while following safety regulations and the local laws, are great ways to connect with nature and the environment while raising your energetic frequency.

Sailing, skiing, or canoeing, generally, will have a higher frequency than running, for example, but if you run while listening to great music and in a beautiful place, the run can then have a very high frequency. Jumping on a trampoline, playing golf or tennis, using a hula hoop, jumping rope, dancing around your bedroom, or working out to a Wii game are fun, good ways to increase your energetic frequency. All kinds of physical activity can increase your frequency if you enjoy it and do it with a positive attitude, with a smile on your face.

# Open Eye: The Power of Thought

To a large extent, how high your energy field goes depends on the quality of the thoughts you're thinking in your daily life and while you engage in the sorts of activities listed above. If you had to describe your typical mood or attitude in a word or two, what would it be? Do you tend to be angry? Critical? Nervous? Tired? Frustrated? Impatient? Stressed out? Worried? Sarcastic? Gossipy? Lecherous? Jealous and competitive? What is your unconscious go-to emotional state when you're driving around town, mowing the lawn, or doing the dishes? Pay attention to the emotional flow running in the background of your being and then be honest with yourself about whether or not it needs changing.

You can be swimming at a gorgeous beach, but if your thoughts are complaining and negative, the experience and resultant frequency will be diminished, perhaps even moving you into the negative range despite the lovely setting. You can be out for a nice dinner at a restaurant, but if you're annoyed with the server, you're just not going to have as much fun on your evening out. You can be going to your friend's birthday party, but if you're worried that your shoes don't match your dress, that you're not having a "good hair day," or if you're concerned that you're not a great dancer, you're going to severely limit how much fun you will have at the party. Instead, put on some clothes that feel comfortable or decide that any shoes that don't hurt your feet are the perfect shoes, mess your hair up a bit more on purpose, and then go dance around like an idiot and have a blast!

You can follow an exercise video in your cramped and dusty living room, and if you're laughing and upbeat, your mood and energy will be greatly elevated. As you begin to practice shifting and selecting your frequency state you will realize that it largely under your control and that external circumstances have little-to-no effect on how you feel or on the frequency at which you resonate-unless you let them.

Chances are pretty good that your mind is busy most of the time, flitting from one thought to another, churning words about in your head. Before you get good at releasing or stilling your thoughts, it is critical to learn how to choose them. All of them. Consciously, and with care.

The quality of your thinking and the content of your thoughts are the single greatest determiner (barring warfare, plague, or other forms of extreme danger, hardship, or deprivation) of the quality of your life. Even in life-threatening situations, if you can maintain a really high frequency, your intuition will also be high and you'll likely be able to sense where to go or not go, what to do or not do, what to say, and be given anything else you need to create the best possible outcome for yourself and others.

Choose positive, encouraging, kind, supportive, optimistic thoughts toward yourself and others and about the world; clear, raise, and heal your energy and in the process you will draw more and more positive people and experiences into your life.

Pay attention to your thoughts. Do you like them? If your thoughts suddenly came to life before you in this instant, would they make you happy? Would they frighten or upset you? Would they create danger or hardship for you?

I want to repeat the preceding comment in order to more fully draw your attention to it. Again, if the thoughts you're thinking right now were to suddenly manifest in your life as you entertained them, what would happen? This idea is one worth spending significant time with. If you don't like the content of your thoughts, don't think those kinds of thoughts. It's your head. It's your mind. Put some love and kindness in there. Show some respect for your life and its purpose. Decide to become the proctor of your thinking. As soon as you notice them, immediately remove fearful and destructive thoughts from your mind and replace them with ones that support happiness and optimism.

If your thoughts are negative, fearful, judgmental, cranky, complaining, or otherwise destructive, they are lowering your energy as you think them. They will also contribute to a lowering of the energy frequencies of the people around you, even if this occurs unconsciously or only reduces their frequency temporarily. By thinking noxious thoughts, you're not only making yourself less happy, less peaceful, and contributing to poorer health for yourself, you're not doing the rest of the world any great favors either.

The single most important action that people can practice is to become more conscious of the thoughts they're thinking and then to delete the negative, unhelpful ones from their minds, instead selecting positive, healing, and uplifting thoughts to think.

# The Third Eye: Turning Negative Thoughts into Positive Affirmations

Perhaps you had a harsh thought about your boss, calling him names silently under your breath. Don't leave those negative thoughts unchallenged to roam free in your mind. That negativity will take over your mental landscape and supplant the peace and joy you could be feeling with judgment, harshness, and regret. Instead, replace the old, stale, unpleasant thoughts with ones that support the good and the beautiful in your life and in the lives of others.

Here are a few sample examples of possible thought "turn-arounds":

Your old thought:   "That boyfriend was a jerk."

New thought:   "May God grant him peace and happiness. May God help me find peace within."

Your old thought: "My boss is a disorganized, incompetent mess."

New thought: "Thank you for my job. May I approach each day with a willingness to learn, to grow, and to be of service."

Your old thought: "People are so inconsiderate. They throw trash out of their car windows and blow smoke in my face."

New thought: "Dear God, please help me be more thoughtful of others. Help me be kind to them. Please help all of us to heal and know peace."

Your old thought: "I hate that TV show. It's an insult to women and to the entire species."

New thought: "I choose to turn off the TV right now and to find other ways to occupy my time constructively. Instead, I choose to read fun books, exercise, play music, spend time with positive people, meditate, learn something new, and develop a fun hobby."

Your old thought:    "This city has some of the worst drivers in the world! What a bunch of idiots! I'll be lucky to get out of here alive, never mind to actually get where I'm going."

New thought:    "The driving feels tricky today. I'd better hang up the phone, turn off the radio, and really concentrate. Dear God, please help me and all those around me be safe, careful, helpful, thoughtful drivers. Bless everyone in this city with long life and perfect health."

Your old thought:    "I can't believe she said that! What a jerk!"

New thought: "She must be scared or having a bad day. God bless her." Internally, in this case, you send peace and compassion to the person who is being unkind to you. At the same time, you might feel invited to gently challenge the statements by saying something along the lines of, "Is everything okay? Are you all right?" You might feel that you're meant to draw a firmer boundary by stating something along the lines of, "Please don't speak to me that way. I want to hear what you have to say, but I don't want to be called names."

You might also feel an invitation to simply remain quiet and internally utter gentle prayers for that person. In any case, mentally release the emotional charge and any hurt from your mind and body. You also want to be sure that you aren't also speaking in an unkind way toward the other person. Did you instigate this? Are you participating? If that's the case, you'll need to own that pattern in yourself. If, however, you're interacting with someone who is often verbally and/or emotionally abuse and doesn't require the slightest provocation to behave in this manner, listen within and select one of the responses from those mentioned above. In any case, you're responsible for your own thoughts and want to shift them into the positive, wise, loving, and supportive range. That choice, daily, is up to you.

Your old thought: "The world is falling apart. People are killing each other. Politicians are greedy, corrupt liars."

New thought: "God bless all governments at the local, state, federal, and international levels. Help us to be kind, generous, and peaceful. Help us to vote and participate in the world wisely and with compassion for others. Help us to serve our brothers. Help us to pray and meditate every day so that we may develop a deep sense of peace within ourselves and in our lives. May all conflict, internal, in the home and in relationships, at work and in neighborhoods, in countries and around the world, now end. Help us awaken from this nightmare and choose peace instead."

Every negative thought can be turned around. All complaining or harsh thinking can be replaced by kind or neutral thoughts instead. You'll feel a lot better if you remove the negative rant from your head. At the same time, you'll release the biggest obstacle to clearing and raising your energy and to being able to maintain a high frequency energy pattern within yourself and toward the lives that surround you, and with minimal effort.

Also, you'll become a much better meditator.

These ideas may sound like a lot to go through to simply sit down and meditate! In fact, it isn't necessary to engage in these activities in order to practice Frequency Meditation. Rather, by monitoring your energy frequency and over time working to improve your energy levels, this and all forms of meditation will become more effective and fun.

Learning to meditate means learning to become aware of our own thoughts, taking responsibility for them and selecting them with greater care, and beginning to consciously choose what we want to think about, when, and how.

What we think about creates our moods. What we think about determines what we are attracting into our personal experience. What we think about affects the quality of our lives, our happiness, and our ability to affect positive change in the world.

- Paying attention to your thoughts creates greater awareness and presence.

- Learning to meditate is a choice to become more conscious and aware.

- Learning to meditate involves becoming more present in the moment.

- By monitoring your frequency levels, you'll become more aware of your own patterns of thought and behavior and recognize those activities and situations that support your growth, inner peace, and healing–and those that don't.
- By healing your thinking, you will increase your frequency levels.

- By improving your energetic frequency, you will improve both the content and the quality of your thinking.

- Meditating creates better health and happiness because it heals your mind.

- Given some dedication and practice, meditation will begin to work miracles in your life.

# Chakras: The Thymus Thump

The Thymus Thump is a tapping technique that helps to center and align the body. Additionally, it works to improve one's mood and increase one's energy level. We should probably all do the Thymus Thump in the morning and again during the day whenever we feel an energy slump or if we're starting to get frustrated, fearful, or agitated. I strongly recommend, as well, that you do this exercise for a few moments each time you sit down to meditate.

Your thymus gland lies behind the sternum, located between your lungs, high in the center of your chest not far from your heart. The thymus gland produces T-cells. T-cells are central to having a strong and healthy immune system. The thymus also assists in the flow of lymph in the body. By gently thumping over this area with your hands, a bit like a gorilla, you stimulate this gland and energy center of the body.

The Thymus Thump exercise was developed by Dr. John Diamond and has become a staple among many energy workers as a way to clear, balance, and strengthen the energy systems of the body.

To perform the Thymus Thump, tap firmly but lightly with your fingers tips above the breasts, moving your hands a bit up and down and remembering to take deep, relaxing breaths. If you prefer, you can gently rub this area, making little circles around the sternum with your hands or fingertips. Alternatively, you can thump (not hard!) this area with your fists, alternating your hands as you do so.

To make this exercise even more effective, while you're tapping, smile, think of someone you love, and as you exhale say, "Ha, ha, ha!" I've seen this version of the Thymus Thump demonstrated by Barbara Stone, Ph.D., but whether she developed this upgraded form of the exercise or learned it from someone else, I don't know. I do know that this exercise can be transformative to your mood, balance, and energy levels.

Try the Thymus Thump, or the Thymus Thump combined with smiling and loving thoughts, a few times. Usually about 30-40 seconds is enough time to spend on this exercise.

A way to personalize this exercise is to state positive affirmations while you're thumping gently around the sternum. Examples of possible affirmations could include statements such as, "I love and care for myself," "I am a happy, vibrant, successful person," "Everything in my world is working out perfectly. I embrace God's plan for my life," or "I choose to be happy right now."

If you're a person who is assisted in learning by having a visual demonstration or by being able to listen to someone explain out loud how to do something, please look up some videos online that show you how to do the Thymus Thump.

# Purification: Cross-lateral Exercises

Another great way to align and balance your body and energy systems is by doing some cross-lateral tapping. For these exercises you can imagine a vertical line running down the center of your body. When tapping you're going to cross your right hand over and tap on the left side of your body and then bring your left hand over to the right side of your body in order to tap.

The tapping is relaxed and doesn't require pressure. While you tap, remember to inhale deeply and to mentally let go as you exhale.

One way to tap cross-laterally is to tap on opposite knees, tapping once on the left knee, then once on the right knee, and back and forth for a few alterations. You can do this exercise while sitting down. If you prefer, you can also perform this exercise while standing, in which case you'll lift up the left knee and tap it with your right hand. You'll bring your left leg back to the ground and then lift up your right knee and tap it with your left hand, and so on.

You can tap on opposite shoulders, on the top of the opposite ear, on the opposite side of your rib cage (around the bra line, if wearing a bra is something that you do), or on your opposite hip.

Another version of this exercise involves tapping on the opposite heel. While standing, bend your left leg up behind you and reach behind your back and tap your left heel with your right hand. Now while standing on your left leg, lift up your right leg behind you and tap the right heel with your left hand. Alternate bending each leg up behind you and tapping the heel with the opposite hand. These exercises help to improve your physical balance, an essential part of health and aging gracefully. These exercises also help to balance and clear your system internally.

# Child: Laughter Yoga

Laughter yoga was developed in India by Dr. Madan Kataria in 1995. Like meditation, laughter has been shown to provide a range of health benefits and to reduce stress. In addition, laughter gives your body an aerobic workout and helps to establish and maintain bonds between people. In laughter yoga you decide to start laughing. While at first the laughter may be forced, usually before long you're laughing naturally. With practice, it becomes easier and easier to start laughing simply by deciding to do so.

Laughter yoga is often practiced in groups. As you've probably experienced before, laughter is contagious. If you're meditating with a friend or in a group, lead everyone in a couple of laughter yoga exercises in order to help you raise your energy frequencies before you start to meditate. If you're meditating by yourself, you can still practice laughter yoga before starting your session.

Deliberately choosing to laugh is one of the most effectives methods for increasing energetic levels. In addition to using laughter as a frequency-raiser prior to meditating, you can also use it to help release any resistance that comes up during meditation as you encounter energetic blockages or if you have difficulty raising your frequency while meditating.

As with other techniques described in this book such as muscle testing and the Thymus Thump, there is a lot of information available online to help you learn more about laughter yoga. A quick Internet search will yield a range of articles on the topic. Watching videos on laughter yoga will help you to get started laughing as well. For example, Dr. Kataria has posted a YouTube video with 100 different laughter yoga exercises you can try. Especially if, like me, you tend to meditate by yourself, try watching a few minutes of one of the great YouTube laughter yoga videos available online and spend a little time laughing along. Your energetic frequency will naturally rise, your body will begin to relax, your breathing will open and deepen, and you'll be ready to have a wonderful meditation session.

Then, when you're meditating and resistance occurs, think back to the funny laughter videos you watched and to the people who were laughing. Remembering and visualizing laughter, even that of someone else, should immediately increase your frequency and have you laughing as well.

Many people take their meditation practice very seriously. Some meditation traditions take the teaching and practice of mediation very seriously as well. In some schools of meditation there are strict rules about how to position the body, how to breathe, what one should do with ones eyes, whether or not one is allowed to move or change positions while meditating, and so on. If you're part of one of the strict, rigorous meditation practices and you find that it works wonderfully for you, that's great. Continue on that journey. However, if you've picked up this book you might be interested in and open to other approaches to meditation.

Frequency Meditation does not have any rules. I do recommend that you breathe, but then I'd recommend that to anyone. When practicing Frequency Meditation, sit wherever and however you like, as long as you're comfortable. You might want to take off your shoes or remove a belt if it restricts your movement or breath, but the basic principle is just to relax and make yourself comfortable.

Meditation is an example of one more aspect of our lives in which we can learn to take things less seriously. Meditation can become a key practice in which we also practice releasing controlling thoughts and behaviors, simply letting go and letting ourselves be at ease and just be. If we can learn to take ourselves, our thoughts, and the details of our lives less seriously, our frequencies will begin to soar.

# Karma: How to Do Frequency Meditation

Let's say that you've done some energy exercises and worked on positive thinking, your energy frequency is at 225 or higher, and you decide you're ready to meditate. Sit down somewhere comfortable. I recommend avoiding crossing your arms or legs. Instead, keep your body position open and relaxed. If there's external noise that you can't turn off such as the barking of the neighbor's dog–apparently typing this line was a sort of stage cue for the neighbor's dog, who immediately began to bark–consciously decide that you like this sound.

If there's a crying baby three rows in front of you in the airplane, decide that you're glad that this family is going on a trip and wish them a wonderful time. Send the baby love, peace, and comfort. Affirm that every time the dog barks or the baby cries, you feel more peaceful, centered, and relaxed. Decide that this is so. You're in charge of your life. You're getting used to telling your mind both what and how to think. You're deciding how you want to view the world and how you want to feel, regardless of external forces. So practice. The loud music from the apartment downstairs helps you to relax and enjoy your day. Affirm it. Say to yourself something along the lines of:

"Every time a horn honks, I feel more and more relaxed."

"Each time there is a siren in the city, I wish everyone health and safety and feel peaceful and centered. My heart rests in God."

"Whenever tires screech I hear the music of the city and rejoice in this moment. I am so thankful for my life."

"Every time I hear someone speaking loudly on the phone in the office down the hall, I feel more rested and calm."

"The hammering and drilling from the construction work outside makes me think of progress. I am safe, happy, and at ease."

"Every time the lady sitting in the booth behind me guffaws and snorts, I give thanks for all of the friendship and joy in the world. I choose to be happy, peaceful, and successful in all that I do."

"Whenever I become aware of potential distractions, I become more focused, effective, centered, and relaxed."

Tell yourself that each time you hear noise, your energy gets clearer and goes up higher. Remind yourself that you feel great and that you welcome this moment just as it is, including all that it contains. If you're feeling daring and want to really embrace this practice, decide that you absolutely love barking dogs and crying babies. Nothing could make you happier. Give thanks to them for filling your life with their music, with their sweetness. Relax, enjoy the sounds all around you and affirm that you have everything you need, that your life is unfolding perfectly and according to plan, and that you are happy. Thank God for all of the gifts in your life and settle again quietly into your chair.

Take some slow, relaxing, deep breaths. As you breathe in, repeat to yourself a word that makes you feel more positive such as "joy," "peace," "love," or "kindness." As you breathe out, repeat "I welcome peace," "I am willing to forgive," "I am filled with love," "I love myself and my life," or some other completely positive message. Let your breathing get softer and softer, more and more peaceful. If you're ready to do so, let go of the words you were using to accompany each breath. Now just breathe quietly with your eyes closed.

Consciously let your body relax. Check your frequency now. It should have gone up, at least somewhat, from when you started. If it hasn't gone up or if it has even moved downwards, affirm, "I completely release all obstacles and fears in this moment. I choose to trust in God. I deserve peace and happiness."

Take some more relaxing breaths. Notice the feel of your bare feet on the cool floor or soft carpet. Notice the support the chair you're sitting on gives your body, holding you up so that sitting requires no effort of any kind on your part. Observe the world around you while sitting with your eyes closed. Is there a light breeze? Is the room warm or cool? Are birds singing nearby?

Whatever is going on around you, give thanks for it, welcome it, and then let it go from your mind. Check your frequency again.

Continue to check, relax, breathe, and release all sense of tightness, of restriction in your breath or body. Affirm, "Meditating is easy and relaxing." Tell yourself, "I enjoy meditating" or "I'm having fun sitting in peace."

Check your frequency. By now it may well have ascended to the 400s. Regardless of the frequency you're currently at, begin to tell yourself that your energy is rising as you sit here quietly. If you're at 410, now affirm "425." If you're at 200, affirm "210." Relax and breathe for a few moments, releasing all thoughts and concerns. Now affirm "235" or "440" or whatever number comes to your mind that is a little bit higher than the level where you were a few moments before.

Repeat this process until you're at a number that gives you a sense of quiet and peace. Inexperienced meditators might have as a goal to meditate at frequency 350. If you've been used to cycling a bit above or below 200, raising your energy to 350 will feel like a huge gift. You may discover that you feel better than you have in quite some time. Continue to practice bringing your energy system up to 350, even when you're not meditating. Get used to what it feels like to live your daily life from a higher frequency pattern. Learn to feel relaxed and comfortable at this higher energy state. Notice how it is getting easier and easier to arrive at 350.

You'll soon find that not only is it becoming easier to raise up your frequency level, you're beginning your meditation practice at a higher number as well. If perhaps when you sat down to meditate before you would often be around 205, now you might start out at 220 or 230. That's a tremendous increase in frequency. Congratulate yourself on a job well done! Keep practicing and getting more and more comfortable rising up to and sitting in the 300s.

Once you're comfortable getting to, say, 350, and it no longer feels challenging to get to this frequency or to sit there quietly for a while, experiment with raising the energy field at which you meditate a bit higher. Try out 352. Can you sit comfortably at that rate? How about 355? How does that feel? Once you're able to move yourself up to the new, somewhat higher frequency fairly quickly and easily when you sit down to meditate, raise the bar again. Now practice at 360 for a few days. You'll know when you're ready to move up again.

If you consider yourself to be an experienced and successful meditator, try to raise your energy up to at least 510. Practice sitting silently at this frequency each time you meditate. Don't rush yourself. Get comfortable here at 510. You might want to occupy this frequency during meditation for a few days, weeks, or months. You'll probably feel great because by the time you get to frequency 510 because your mind will be much quieter. You should feel peaceful. You may be aware of your body as an energy field. Your limbs might feel more full and present. Your breathing should come easily and feel like it's nourishing your entire body. You might see colors in your mind.

Frequency 510 is a sort of magical number. 500 is the beginning of the spiritual range, and by 510 you are firmly centered in a spiritual, rather than a material, awareness.

The world is busy, material, and dense. It tends to focus on the physical, on the acquisition of necessary or pretty possessions, on beautifying its physical form, and on looking at and questing after the physical forms of other people. This is the world under frequency 500, and the lower you go, the denser this attachment to physicality and materiality becomes. The 300s have a far greater focus on money, possessions, and physical desirability than the 400s. People who live in the 400s might very well have more money, more great possessions, look better, feel healthier and more energetic, and even have more sex, but they're far less obsessed about it than those who tend to spend much of their time at lower frequencies.

The 200s are far more focused on material gain, physical entertainment, and pleasure than the 300s. In the 200s people might want to drink a lot on the weekends to suppress the lower frequencies that are still highly active and that are exercising a fairly constant pull on their systems. They might work out often in order to feel a jolt of higher energy. There's more insecurity in the 200s than in the 300s. People in the 200s need a lot more external validation from other people to feel okay. They may want to be noticed or admired on a regular basis, engaging in activities that will garner them attention (both of the positive and the negative variety) or approval. They might seek out compliments for the way they dress or how they look, what they own, or whom they know.

All of this is fine. It's perfect to be wherever you are at a given moment. Eventually you want to learn to be conscious and comfortable at all frequencies. For now, you're learning to regulate your thoughts and energy levels. You're noticing the qualities of the different frequencies, what they feel like in your body and how they inhabit your thoughts and your mind. You're beginning to realize that you can choose which frequencies best suit a given activity or will support the way you want to think and feel at that time. In every moment you're actively, although perhaps largely unconsciously, making a choice about how you want to feel and the energy frequencies and quality of life you're going to experience.

Frequency Meditation is teaching you to observe, to become more conscious, and to deliberately select the frequency at which you want to sit in meditation and, increasingly, that you want to inhabit as you move through the world.

By frequency 510 you know that you are okay. You can feel your inner worth without effort. You're aware that life has a purpose and that everyone has a part to play in the world. You feel more relaxed and trusting of life and in the unfolding of your path in this lifetime.

Again, it might be helpful and healthy for you to practice meditating at frequency 510 for a few days or even for a few months. When you feel ready, you can try out meditation at somewhat higher frequencies by affirming "515," "520," or "530," working your way up gradually to whatever higher frequency feels right to you.

# Walking: Becoming Grounded After Each Frequency Meditation Session

It is the goal of this method, as with all meditation techniques, to still the mind and quiet the inner voice that dominates the thinking of most people, most of the time. Thinking begins to become calmer as one enters the 400s. In the 400s there are occasional pauses in one's internal dialogue, brief gaps in the internal conversation and in automatic, compulsive thinking. Those quiet gaps allow our higher mind and thinking, as well as wisdom from realms beyond ourselves, to enter the space, however brief, left by the silence.

It is not until frequency 500 or above that the mind truly has the capacity to enter the silence. At this point, increasingly long stretches of quiet and peace may be experienced. The calm in this range is both energizing and healing. Beginning at 500 on the Hawkins scale, one is in the spiritual realm, more connected to experiences and ideas of a spiritual nature. As you begin to practice Frequency Meditation, you may soon find yourself meditating at frequency 500 or above.

When one finishes a Frequency Meditation session, it is essential to become centered and grounded again. It is particularly important to ground oneself in the material reality with which one is surrounded before driving a car or operating any kind of machinery. It is important to remember how the physical world works and to understand how its rules and laws, such as gravity and the traffic system, operate.

In highly effective meditation, one releases most ordinary, material concerns in favor of a connection with the spiritual realm of consciousness that begins at frequency 500. After meditation one must solidly reenter the physical, material realm of daily life in a conscious, deliberate, centered way.

Here are a series of exercises to help you become centered and grounded again after Frequency Meditation. Make sure that your doctor gives you permission to do physical exercise, regardless of how gentle, before beginning any of these grounding practices. Do one or more of them until you feel completely grounded and focused.

Grounding exercises:

- The Thymus Thump.

- Cross-lateral exercises.

- Slowly and gently reach down and touch your toes (or as close as you can get–do these exercises while seated if that's safer and more helpful to you). Now straighten your body and relax your arms at your side. Next, stretch your arms above your head while reaching for the sky. Tilt your head gently backwards and gaze upwards. Return to a relaxed standing position. Now reach your arms out horizontally to your sides. Lean to the right while reaching outwards with your right hand. Return to center. Lean to the left while stretching toward your left with your left arm. Return to center and let your arms hang at your sides. Repeat this series of exercises until you feel fully centered and present.

- Stand erect and consciously lengthen your spine so that you're standing tall with your head facing straight forward, not tilted. Bend your head to the right so that your right ear approaches your right shoulder. Relax and enjoy this gentle stretch. Return your head to the center. Now bend your head to the left so that your left ear approaches your left shoulder. Breathe and feel that easy stretch in your neck. Return your head to the center. Make sure that your chin is not tilted down toward your chest, to one side or another, or upwards, even a little bit, toward the sky. Your chin should point forward as if you were standing at attention.

- Center your awareness in your shoulders and do a few shoulder rolls from front to back and then from back to front. Make sure that your shoulders are straight and even. Consciously think "back" while pulling your shoulders slightly back so that you stand straight and tall. Consciously think "down" while pulling your shoulders downward a bit, correcting any tendency to raise or hunch your shoulders.

- Gently bounce up and down while standing straight, making sure that your knees aren't locked. You don't need to jump, just softly bounce in place. With each downward motion send your focus down into your lower body.

- Focus on breathing calmly and slowly from your belly. With each breath send your energy deep into the earth where you anchor it as if with a long tether. Feel your connection to the earth. Rest for a few moments in this awareness. When you're ready, slowly bring your energy up from the earth and back into your body. Center that earthy energy low in your abdomen. Feel that energy healing your stomach and chest and filling you with peace and well-being.

- Focus on your feet. Become aware of your feet, how they feel, and of the energy moving through them. Feel how your feet touch the floor or the ground. Feel how your feet balance you steadily upon the earth.

- Only do the following exercise if you have good balance and are in good physical condition. The exercise: Balance your energy in your feet.

Now gently rock your body onto the balls of your feet, then onto your heels, then onto your toes before returning to stand with your feet securely on the ground. Next rock your feet onto their right side and hold for a few seconds and then rock onto the left side of your feet and do the same. Now return your stance to a center position, feeling yourself balanced and grounded with your feet steady and flat on the earth.

- Take a short walk around the house, up and down the stairs, down the street, or in a garden or park. Breathe in the fresh air and notice the nature and beauty all around you. If you're at home, be sure to gaze out a window periodically so that you can see trees, flowers, birds, or the sky.

- Do some gardening. Even raking some leaves or pulling a few weeds will help you to reconnect with nature and with the earth.

- An affirmation: State out loud or in your mind, "The earth is my home." Affirm that you belong on this earth and that you are fully at home everywhere on this earth, no matter where you go. Quiet your mind and really feel your connection to the earth, to its seasons, to its weather, to its plants and animals, its rhythms and wisdom, and to its core.

- An affirmation: State out loud or in your mind, "My life is a gift. It belongs to me, and I belong right here, right now." Feel your energy and your body as being fully present in this space and time, in the here and now.

- Do a mundane activity like chopping vegetables, puttering in the garage, vacuuming, dusting, washing the car, paying the bills, doing some laundry, taking a bath, or straightening a room in your home. Try to be as conscious and focused as possible while you're cleaning or taking care of chores.

- As you exhale, sing a long, solid, deep note. Feel the tone resonating within your being, beginning in your throat and chest and then spreading out to the rest of your body and into the room where you're sitting. Repeat this process until you feel fully focused in the moment.

- Imagine a beautiful, light-filled cord or rope extending from above your head, running through the vertical center of your body, and then flowing down deep into the earth. See how this cord helps you to sit and stand straight and tall. Feel how this cord fills you with light. Imagine this cord replenishing your energy, sustaining you with healing light, and filling you with poise, balance, perfect awareness, and peace.

- Picture your body standing firmly within a rectangular prism. With your hands or with your mind, reach out before you and feel the limits of the front of this prism. Now reach out behind you–this is much easier to do as a visualization exercise than by actually stretching your arms behind you–and feel the edges of the prism behind your back. Next reach toward your right to feel where the edges of this energetic prism begin and then feel outwards toward your left and do the same. Finally feel the limits of the prism above and below you with your mind.
If this prism feels too close or tight around you, imagine its strong sides moving outward two or three feet in all directions around you. Imagine the sides of this rectangular prism as being made out of your favorite metal that is shining brightly in the sun or is constructed out of a fine mesh composed of several different metals woven together. Feel your body fully centered, protected, safe, and grounded within this energetic prism.

# Forgiveness: If Meditation Feels Hard for You

If you're having trouble raising your energy level, do it more slowly. We're not in a rush. Meditation is largely about letting go of control. In meditation you stop doing. You're no longer busy, rushing about or working to check off items on the day's to-do list. You're not trying to control yourself and you're not trying to control others. You're learning to gently find a settled and peaceful place within your heart and mind into which you can relax.

During meditation you let go of goal setting, of planning, of organizing and thinking. You're just sitting quietly. You're enjoying the moment in silence. You're practicing simply being.

During meditation you're not thinking, not feeling, and not doing. Release your attention from your feelings. If you need them, you can pay attention to them later. You also release your attention from your thoughts. If they're important, you can listen to them later.

It requires some self-discipline to decide to simply sit still, quietly, with your eyes closed. It requires some willingness to change old patterns and to release old ways of interacting with yourself and with the world. It requires a conscious decision and to choose that you're going to gently and willingly sit with yourself.

- In meditation, you're not trying to change anything.
- In meditation, you're being, not doing.
- In meditation, you're allowing yourself to settle deeply into this moment without arguing with it, without talking to it, without engaging with it in any way.
- In meditation, you're simply present.

If you're having a hard time practicing Frequency Meditation (or, of course, other kinds of meditation), you probably haven't spent enough time in the preparation stage.

Return to Chapter 13, Guided Imagery: Techniques for Increasing Your Frequency, to review ideas for how to raise your energy level. Study the list for a bit. Which items are you already doing? Are you doing them regularly? Are you doing them with a relaxed and positive manner?

What items on the list could you add into your life, at least from time to time? Are you getting some exercise? Are you practicing laughter yoga? Are you doing the exercise in which you exhale while singing out "ahhh?" What else on the list appeals to you?

It's time to expand your interests, your hobbies, and your intellectual life. As I've heard the writer and public speaker Jean Houston say, "If you're always thinking the same thoughts, you're not just boring yourself, you're boring God." (That might not be a verbatim quote, but it's very close.) What variety can you add into your daily life? What sorts of new things can you incorporate into your weekends? Into your thoughts? It's time to become better informed. It's time to entertain some new ideas.

One of the best ways to increase your energy frequency over time is to study and learn new things. Read some books. Read some interesting articles online. Watch some informative videos and documentaries. Develop a new interest or hobby. Develop a new skill. Whether or not these new skills make you more competitive in the job market is not the goal here, although that might be a nice added benefit; new abilities will make you exercise your mind in different ways, helping to improve your energy levels.

Are you constantly releasing negative thinking? This may be the single most important practice for your success. If, like many, many people, your thoughts are predominantly negative and complaining, this pattern needs to shift in order to raise and clear your energy and in order to help you meditate more successfully.

Replacing a negative stance with a positive, optimistic one takes time, vigilance, and practice. However, even simply deciding to become a more positive person and working to replace at least some of your negative thoughts every single day with more uplifting ones will result in a significant shift in your energy and in your life.

# Affirmations: The Technique

Let's assume that with positive thinking, affirmations of gratitude, and loving prayer that your energy level is now around 250 or higher when you sit down to meditate. Relax and focus on gentle, deep breaths that reach into your belly. State, "I am now willing and ready to bring peace to my mind by increasing my energy frequency." Feel that statement as true. Now say, "251." Wait a few moments while affirming the positive word you've selected such as "truth" or "joy" and then think "252." As soon as you feel ready, keep going. Think "253," then pause and breathe. Silently state "254" and think "happy." Next affirm "255, 256, 257, 258" and think of the word "healing." Finally, mentally state "259, 260" and think "truth" or silently affirm other similarly positive, simple words.

At 270, pause for a few moments and flow color through your mind and through and around your body. Whichever color comes to mind (except red, gray, brown, or black), imagine mentally pouring it all over yourself while breathing deeply and sitting peacefully.

Now continue. Silently state, "271, 272, 273, 274." Think "peace" and breathe in more color and then think, "275." Add in some more color and then affirm "276, 277, 278, 279, 280." Once again, rest in silence for a little bit at this frequency and then, when you feel ready, continue to count upwards. If counting up by 1's feels too slow for you, count by 2's or by 5's. If you think that you're ready to move upwards more quickly, then count up faster. Simply state whatever numbers feel right to you as you move up the frequency scale at your own pace.

Whenever you feel a bit of resistance, your mind spaces out, you get distracted, or you start to feel tense, stop right there. The resistance that showed up, in whatever form (tension, anxiety, fatigue, disinterest), is a signal that you've got some stuck energy at that specific frequency.

Take some time at the resistant frequency, say at 281, and just breathe quietly with your eyes closed and practice some positive affirmations in your mind such as:

"I now release all tension."

"I now release all fears."

"I now release all pain from my body and mind.

"I now release all discomfort from my body and mind."

"I choose to be at peace."

"I choose to heal and grow."

"I choose to be happy."

"I'm willing and ready to be happy."

"I'm willing and ready to be at peace."

"I'm willing and ready to be healthy in every way."

"I release the past."

"I release all thoughts of the past."

"I release the future."

"I release all ideas about the future."

"I am present."

"I am safe."

"It is safe to be present."

"It is safe to be here."

"I am surrounded by loving words and deeds."

"I am treated with kindness and respect."

"I am enveloped in the Peace of God."

"I am loved by God."

"All is well."

Use the statements that feel helpful to you. Perhaps one or two in particular with resonate with you as being helpful in the moment. Stick with those for a while until you feel the energy in your body shift or release.

Of course, you don't have to use any of the affirmations listed here. You're welcome to make up your own. Use your intuition when creating your statements. What feels right to you?

Maybe you respond more powerfully to vibration than to language at this frequency. Your higher self knows exactly what it needs to release this blockage.

- Try exhaling "ahhh" while you breathe out a tone or note.

- Try doing some cross-lateral tapping.

- Do the Thymus Thump again for a minute or two.

- Use your mind to send bright colors coursing in and around your body.


- Remember to breathe and to focus on the idea of "letting go."


- Do some laughter yoga exercises.



When you feel ready to move on, continue to move upwards, perhaps returning now to counting by 1's until you reach the next point of resistance.

Even though you might find it frustrating, it's actually really helpful each time you encounter, consciously, a bit of resistance in the body-mind. Uncovering this resistance provides extremely helpful information. There is a part of your being that is stuck at this frequency. Help it to let go, gently, by using the various exercises, visualizations, affirmations, and other activities in this book.

The next day when you sit down to meditate again, pay particular attention to the frequency where you encountered some resistance the last time. How does it feel today? Does that frequency require some more releasing work? Does it feel freer? Focus on that frequency and do some more clearing activities to help the resistance continue to clear.

# Light: Getting to Frequency 300

It might happen right away or it might take a couple of months, but at some point fairly early in your Frequency Meditation practice you'll probably discover that you're now at frequency 300. Frequency 300 isn't just 10 times higher than frequency 299, the way 299 is ten times higher than 298. Getting to 300 also represents a shift in your way of thinking and being. A similar shift occurs when you reach frequencies 400 and 500. Each time you begin a new range of frequencies, a significant shift is occurring.

We've already talked at some length about the enormous shift that occurs at frequency 200, so I won't go into it again here. Arriving at frequencies 300 and 400 also represent an important change in goals, motivation, outlook, and ways of interacting with the world. They're huge shifts, but they're not as ground-changing as getting to 200, the beginning of the healthy and positive range of energies, nor are they as monumental as getting to 500, the beginning of the spiritual dimension on earth.

As you get near 300, starting at the end of the 200s and continuing into the beginning of the 300s, pay close attention to how you feel. Be on the lookout for any resistance you feel, whether in your body, in your mind, or to this material and to meditating in general. Be sure to spend plenty of time doing some extra releasing work by selecting those exercises that most appeal to you in the moment.

How much time is plenty of time? It might take five minutes to feel clear around this frequency range or you might need to clear the frequency around 300 (or 400, etc.) over a period of a few days, weeks, or months each time you sit down to meditate.

At 300 pause and select the color that comes to your mind (again, except for red, black, brown, or gray) to flow in and all around your body. Let the color settle into your organs and cells. Imagine the color washing over you from head to toe and then flowing away from you and down into the earth for purification.

Once you've finished doing this exercise with one color, let another color come to mind and then begin the exercise again. If you like, you can also work with combinations of colors, ribbons of colors, or the entire rainbow. Red, when combined with the rest of the rainbow hues, is extremely helpful at clearing out old blockages. Red, when used by itself or if combined with black, will be less helpful or may even serve to reinforce the stuck energy in your system.

When you're ready to continue your meditation work, gradually count upwards from 300 or wherever you are at the moment and affirm positive words and statements. Keep your mind and body relaxed and remember to take easy breaths, imagining breathing in from somewhere around your belly button. You can visualize the breath entering and leaving your body from your belly button itself if that is helpful.

If this is enough energy clearing and releasing work for that day, stop here. If you feel ready to continue, keep going.

# Zen: Clearing Resistance

If you feel resistance building, use some of the following exercises to help clear and release the blockage of energy in your system around that frequency. Notice how or where you feel the resistance.

Does the resistance take physical form? Maybe you feel butterflies in your stomach, itching in your back, or discomfort in your legs or neck. Maybe you just can't get your body into a comfortable sitting position. Perhaps you feel an overwhelming need to take a nap. Do clearing work around that feeling of tiredness or around any bodily sensation that is making itself known to your awareness.

Does the resistance have an emotional component? Are you feeling anxious, irritated, impatient, sad, or frustrated? Are feelings of guilt rising to the surface? Imagine those feelings coming to your attention because they're ready to be released. It's time to let them go. Affirm something along the lines of "I am ready and willing to release all of these emotions. I am ready and willing to let go of the past." When you're ready to continue, practice some of the exercises listed below.

Can the resistance be described as mental, as repetitive thoughts running through your mind, or as over-thinking? Are you having an intellectual argument with what you're doing, with this book, or with a word, phrase, or idea that has been presented here or that keeps popping up in your mind? Do you find yourself wanting to argue with the author? Are you having a disagreement in your head with someone you know, with a family member, friend, or coworker? Do you find yourself pointing out the mistakes that other people make? Are you feeling critical? Do you want more precision when talking to other people? Do you tend to rehash details of things that you did, read, or heard? Do you correct people when they speak to you or do you otherwise argue with the world around you?

Other forms of mental resistance can involve coming up with items that require your attention at the moment–the "to-do list" method of resistance.

Thinking that meditation is a waste of time, telling yourself that you have better things to do, and other kinds of inner dialogue are all forms of mental resistance.

Here are some techniques you can use to release resistance and to come back to sufficient stillness and inner readiness before resuming mediation:

- Smile to yourself.

- Give thanks to God for this moment.

- Affirm with calm conviction that you are happy, peaceful, and well.

- Mentally swirl a color or colors in and around your body.

- Perform the "Thymus Thump."

- Do some cross-lateral exercises.

- Laugh, using a technique from laughter yoga.

- Say "ahhh" while exhaling with a tone such as the note C.

- State positive words as you breathe.

- Let the feelings, physical discomfort, and/or mental conversation simply exist. They just are.

Just because they exist doesn't make them interesting, doesn't mean that you have to engage with them, doesn't require that you think about them for even another moment. Don't fight the discomfort. Don't talk to it. Don't disagree with it. Just notice the emotions, thoughts, and sensations and allow them to be.

- Alternatively, encourage the emotions, thoughts, and sensations to course through your body. Be really aware of them as you help them to flow everywhere. Continue to breathe, to affirm positive statements, and to run colors through your body as you intensify and embrace these thoughts and feelings.

Allow yourself to feel the discomfort or resistance and know that it is okay. As you stay with the feelings, they'll either release or increase. If they release, then simply continue on with your meditation, breathing while affirming your word or words and slowly increasing the number that you state as your current frequency.

If the discomfort you're feeling increases, welcome it even though it might scare you and even though it might feel really hard to just sit with those feelings. Let them flow through your body and mind without resistance. Don't talk to them or engage with them–just experience them without response or comment. If you start to vibrate, just let your body shake for a bit. Wrap each uncomfortable thought in a gauzy layer of color; envelop every part of your body that feels anxious, tight, or frantic in beautiful, swirling light. As you breathe in, say, "thank you." Hum a continuous note as you exhale. Keep practicing the observing, the allowing, the feeling, and the releasing until the fear or discomfort is fully resolved.

You will be amazed at how much freer you feel after doing these exercises. As the saying goes, "What you resist, persists," so instead of resisting, allow, embrace, and accept. Then layer upon layer of emotional debris and physical holding begin to exit from your system, never to return.

# Transcendental: Releasing

Here are some more techniques for clearing and releasing stuck energy frequencies and inner or mental resistance to moving forward. Don't rush through these. As you continue to practice Frequency Meditation, make sure that you work with each of these at least once.

- Place your hands over your sternum and invite in divine, healing light. Ask the light to fill your thymus with healing and blessings. Request that this light continue on from your thymus to go on to energize and bless all of your body and mind.

- Invite in God's angels and ask them to help you clear and balance your energy system. Ask them to help you meditate and heal. Thank them for their blessings, love, and support.

- Focus your mind in your feet. Really become aware of your feet, how they touch the ground, how they feel, and whether they're warm or cold. Let your awareness expand in and around your feet. What do you notice? Just feel it. Allow your awareness to surround and infuse your feet. As you become more and more centered in the sensations of your feet, feel their strong connection to the earth and how this connection is helping you to feel calm, centered, and grounded. Remember to breathe from your belly.

- Bring your attention to your shoulders. Most people hold at least some tension in this area of their body. How do your shoulders feel? Are they tight? Bunched up? Slumped? Raised? Imagine your shoulders releasing all of the tension they're carrying. Imagine water flowing over and around them, taking all tension and worry along with it. See your shoulders become more flexible. Imagine them feeling light, relaxed, and free. With each exhale allow tension to flow down from your shoulders and into the center of the earth.

- Bring your attention to your breath. There are a number of different ways to clear energy with the breath. You can pull in a positive concept into your mind during the in breath such as "love" and release a negative one such as "fear" on the out breath. You can affirm a positive idea such as "peace" during both the in breath and the out breath. You can visualize the air entering your body as white light that circulates throughout your system, bringing with it healing and clarity. You can feel your breath as a beautiful pattern of energy that flows in circuits through your body. See this energy pattern as wise, full of kindness, relaxing, and as designed by God.

# Journey: Becoming Proficient at Frequency Meditation

As you get more and more comfortable with this form of meditation, you'll soon be able to count upwards more quickly. Instead of moving upwards one point at a time (which is actually a lot–remember that each point upwards represents ten times more energy), you might now count upwards by 5's, going from 280 to 285 to 290, and so on. Don't forget to stop and do the clearing work whenever you feel stuck or like you're avoiding moving forward or resisting your meditation practice.

Soon you'll be counting upwards by 10's or 20's. In order to make sure that you're clearing all of the frequencies completely, clearing every single point along Hawkins' energy scale (this may need to happen just once or there may be specific frequencies that you need to clear over and over again), be sure to sometimes move upwards by 6's or 7's, and so on. In this way, you could start counting at 300, and then continue counting by 6's to 306, 312, 318, 324, etc. If you have trouble doing math in your head, decide what you're going to do in advance and then write out the numbers sequentially that you're going to use for this particular meditation. Look at each number in turn and affirm that you're now resonating at that frequency. Pause and let that energy signature flow through your being, bringing healing and clearing with it. Whenever you need to pause longer, do so. If you need to do some of the exercises described above, practice them until that energy pattern feels released and you sense that you have permission to move forward to the next number. Close your eyes again in between stating each number to help you still your mind and your thinking and to avoid becoming distracted by external images.

After a while when you sit down to meditate, your internal "default setting" or "set point," the frequency number that you tend to hang out at much of the time from day to day, will begin to rise up higher and higher. Whereas before you had to work to get your energy level over 200 or up to 250 so that you felt ready to start meditating each day, now perhaps when you tune into your system, you discover that you usually are around 275. Before you know it, your default frequency has climbed to 290, and so on.

Not only will your internal frequency increase over time but you'll also soon find that it becomes easier and easier to raise your frequency levels.

For example, if you now typically begin to meditate at 285, when you start to state higher numbers, you're able to move upwards much more quickly, comfortably, and easily. Before you know it you may find that it only takes a few minutes to get to frequency 510. This shift will be an indication that you're ready to now plateau at a higher number when meditating, perhaps spending the heart of your meditation session at frequency 525 or 540.

# Visualization: Examples of Frequency Meditation Sessions

Here are some examples of what Frequency Meditation can involve. Again, you are going to first check your frequency level with muscle testing and then you'll periodically quickly check it again to see where you are on the scale. As you read through these sample Frequency Meditation sessions, take your time and really feel the words, images, and frequencies resonating in your mind and in your body. You may feel inspired to try out some of these models for yourself. One a day is plenty, and I recommend using the same template for your meditation for several days in a row, but follow your intuition and do what feels right and best to you. Don't forget to use some of the grounding exercises when you're done meditating.

Remember that there is neither a sense of urgency nor a rushing to complete a chapter or page as you read this. You're relaxed, centered, and aligned with the higher messages and frequencies presented here.

The following is an example of what this inner dialogue could look like:

250. (A starting point.)

Relaxing my mind and breathing deeply.

Peace to my mind.

Peace to my heart.

Peace to my body.

275.

Calm.

Gentle heart.

280.

Breathing in with the word "peace" and breathing out with the word "open" for a cycle of 20 or so breaths. (There's no need to count them. Just do this until you feel a subtle shift, then move on.)

310.

Openness.

Open heart and open mind.

I am ready and willing to heal my mind with peace.

Peace to my being.

320.

I now choose to release all thinking.

I turn within in silence.

325.

Joy.

(Now the meditator could consciously begin to affirm that his or her frequency is increasing steadily and automatically, or else he or she can continue to state the frequencies out loud or within the mind, pausing periodically in order to give his or her system a chance to fully calibrate at the next level.)

350.

Peace.

375.

Calm.

400.

Quiet.

410.

Truth.

450.

Silence.

475.

Trust.

495.

Rest.

510.

Happy.

535.

Love.

540.

Perfect health.

550.

Perfect being.

560.

Faith.

575.

Trust in God.

600.

Silence.

At this point, the meditator will just sit quietly for a time, enjoying the deep sense of peace, contentment, and fulfillment embodied at this frequency. Don't worry if you settle into your meditative state around 340, 380, 420, or 450. You don't need to get over 500 in order to meditate successfully. As long as you spend some time at frequency 250 or higher, you will receive some of the benefits of meditation. With time and practice, the higher, quieter, and more peaceful states will be easier to attain, but start where you are and embrace your meditative experience however it shows up and without resistance. Be patient and compassionate with yourself.

Here is another example of what an inner dialogue during Frequency Meditation could look like:

210.

I choose to know peace.

225.

I want to forgive.

250.

This works.

255.

I open my heart.

270.

Breathe in with the word "freedom" and breathe out with the word "release" for a cycle of at least 20 breaths.

290.

My body is relaxed.

310.

My mind is open.

320.

God, I give you all of my fears.

335.

I choose peace.

360.

Quiet.

375.

380.

390.

395.

God is good.

410.

Stillness.

425.

I am peace.

440.

I release my need to think.

445.

450.

455.

Silence.

At this stage, the meditator would simply sit quietly for a while and enjoy feeling more relaxed, centered, and at ease. For someone who began the meditation session around level 210, reaching 455 for a while is an enormous achievement. When they're done meditating they should be able to carry a large measure of the peace and gentleness that they experienced during meditation with them throughout the rest of the day.

Here is a third example of what a Frequency Meditation session might look like:

385.

I am loved.

390.

God is love.

400.

Love surrounds me.

405.

Love protects me.

410.

God, I give thanks.

425.

Thank you for the gift of my life.

430.

I know peace.

440.

I know truth.

450.

I know.

475.

I am God's child.

480.

I live in God's light.

490.

I welcome God's love.

500.

I am God's love.

510.

I am.

540.

Healing.

550.

Healing is love.

560.

I am love.

580.

Love.

590.

Truth.

600.

610.

I am that I am.

620.

Joy.

635.

I am peace.

640.

Stillness.

Remember that each person will begin and end at a different point, making brief rest stops at the frequency levels that they're releasing and clearing in order to ascend higher. Not only will each meditation session look very different from person to person, but each individual's meditation will vary from day to day depending upon how they feel when they start, what's going on in their lives at the moment, and a range of other factors. These influencing factors do not need to be known, figured out, or even glimpsed. Just start where you start and gently proceed forward from there.

Each day will be a bit different, and each meditator's experience will have its own pattern. Having said that, as you become a more accomplished meditator, your meditation sessions and those of other practiced meditators will look more and more similar as you begin to move more fully into the shared, universal, and eternal aspects of higher meditation. In addition, with practice you will usually begin each meditation session at a higher frequency and will then move up to the desired meditation frequency quickly and with ease, whether it be to 490, 520, 560, 610, 700, or some other point.

Soon you won't need to count upwards along the frequency levels while you're meditating. Instead, your system will just glide up along the frequency scale as you relax into meditation. Before long you won't need to focus on your breathing at all. You won't need to silently utter helpful words or phrases such as "joy" or "peace to my heart." You will have learned how to enter the silence, you will have deepened and expanded your sense of stillness within yourself, and you will have made a strong and lasting connection to universal peace and oneness. Eventually, gliding up the energetic continuum will happen effortlessly and with very little thought or conscious engagement with the process at all.

Once you're used to living most of your life in the 400s, a highly effective, positive, and inspired range, you should be able to meditate and reach your desired frequency goal almost immediately.

# Koan: Advanced Frequency Meditation

Your meditation sessions, when beginning around frequency 450 or higher, might then look like this:

450.

Relax.

480.

Kindness.

500.

Peace.

525.

Truth abides in light.

540.

Wholeness.

555.

Perfect health.

590.

Wisdom.

600.

I am joy.

610.

Forgiveness flows from God's heart to mine.

630.

God is in my mind.

650.

I am free.

675.

Perfect stillness.

710.

Silence.

Here's another example of a meditation session of someone highly practiced at Frequency Meditation:

490.

Health and happiness.

510.

I am love.

545.

I resonate health.

570.

Angels surround me.

599.

I choose joy.

625.

Clarity of mind.

677.

My heart is kind.

695.

Love itself.

699.

God is love.

700.

God's will is mine.

720.

The peace of God.

As you move higher up the frequency scale in advanced meditation, the words you state (such as "I am love") might be whispered in your mind, almost without substance at all. You might not need more than a couple of words to help you focus and reach your goal. You might not need any words or phrases at all, choosing to affirm progressive numbers instead. You might simply think "Frequency Meditation" when you sit down to meditate and immediately enter the desired state without resorting to the symbolism of numbers and words. Lean into the stillness and let go. That might be enough.

# Crystal: Rapid Frequency Meditation

I know meditators who meditate for half an hour or more twice a day. Other meditators meditate for an hour or more at a time, whether as part of a daily practice or on the weekends when they have more time. During retreats and workshops, two or three consecutive days might be entirely dedicated to meditation with fellow practitioners. Committing large chunks of time to meditation might be helpful when one is still learning how to meditate. However, once you become accomplished at Frequency Meditation, you'll discover that you can enter a range of high, restful, peaceful frequencies with ease. Your mind immediately becomes quiet. Your thoughts silence themselves. Your body relaxes and you feel an overflowing sense of peace, stillness, and well-being.

Once you've learned how to enter a meditative state in the high 600s or low 700s, the time you dedicate to meditating on a daily basis can now be very brief. By the time you can enter these high frequency states, you can probably enter them rapidly. With clients who are accustomed to meditating or who have done a lot of clearing work around the lower frequencies, including the releasing work of difficult emotional patterns and blockages, I can help guide them into the 610-730 range within moments.

These high frequency states are extremely restful. Just spending a couple of minutes in this elevated range is refreshing and energizing. If you're feeling tired at work or are having trouble focusing, try jumping up to these frequencies briefly and then returning to work on the task at hand. After your quick meditation break (much healthier and more refreshing than a smoking break), continue to maintain yourself in the 350-499 range to invigorate your system and in order to stimulate great bursts of energy and creativity.

If you've learned, through dedication and practice, how to enter these lofty energy states, meditation now takes almost no time at all. It becomes an easy and accessible tool to help you clear your thinking and emotions. Meditation within the high frequency patterns creates deep relaxation and helps to develop internal emotional and psychological stability. High frequency meditation works to rejuvenate your body and energy fields and to bring peace, almost instantaneously, into your life.

Once this ease in entering high frequency states begins to happen for you, you'll probably discover that 4-5 minutes in this state is plenty. Of course, you could stay in these high frequency states for much longer, but most of the time it won't be necessary. Just a few minutes (or as little as a couple of minutes) spent in this state of elevated awareness should leave you feeling refreshed, calm, and clear-headed. You enter the state of eternal peace, envelop your mind in calm stillness, relax, and then return to your daily life, bringing with you a sense of ease, flow, and purpose.

When you enter these still and peaceful states, the calm, poise, and wisdom that you experienced there will follow you back, at least somewhat, into your regular life, actions, and interactions. If you now return to spending time with family and friends, you will find that your relationships are more harmonious, gentle, and easy. The people around you will tend to settle down, focus better, and be more positive and cooperative. Your relationships will become smoother and kinder as you become more accomplished in your meditation practice.

If you now return to your work, ideas will begin to flow and your output will be more focused, organized, clear, and effective. In fact, over time the quality of your work will increase–exponentially. Your entire life will begin to run more effectively and with less effort, your thinking will be more creative and inspired, and your emotions will level off if in the past you tended toward emotional highs and lows.

You are now elevated by the more refined and serene realms with which you were in contact during meditation, and the activities you return to in your life and the relationships with which you're involved will begin to shift as well toward a higher frequency pattern. As you develop a consistent Frequency Meditation practice or other successful meditation regimen in which you enter high energy states of great clarity and stillness, whatever you choose to do is now touched by the gentle wisdom of that range of frequencies. The spiritual essence from those high frequency states that surround us all has become an accessible source for inspiration, healing, and higher truth in your daily life because you are now in regular contact with them. The higher frequency realm is comprised of a loving presence and calm awareness that we have lost sight of by becoming distracted, and even consumed, by the noise and busyness of the world, by the chaotic emotions and the ego-driven concerns of the lower frequency states.

# Standing: Additional Guidelines for Frequency Meditation

When practicing Frequency Meditation, you can use any short word or phrase that you like as long as it is completely positive, encouraging, and feels like the truth for you. If you discover that you don't need to use a word or words periodically while meditating to help you refocus your mind and to help you raise your frequency, then don't use them. The words and phrases are not necessary; they're not required. They're just offered here as potential aids. Following is a list of possible words and phrases that might be useful during Frequency Meditation and that might help you stay on track.

A bit of space is provided here for you to add words and statements that appeal to you. If you do find that words are helpful during Frequency Meditation, you can use a few of them or even repeat the same couple of words to yourself. More isn't necessarily better. Neither is less. It's all up to you.

Here are some words you might find useful in your practice:

Love, joy, truth, peace, nurturing, safety, stillness, calm, protection, forgiveness, honor, kindness, quiet, healing, gentleness, wisdom, generosity, care, optimism, release, happiness, thanks, warmth, positivity, grounded, courage, openness, spirit, boldness, laughter, centered, heaven, balanced, connected, in tune, intuitive, angelic guidance, divine grace, perfect health, soul, blessings, positivity, eternity, letting go, friendliness, perfection, compassion, angels, wholeness, insight, gratitude, presence, aliveness, knowing, softness, silence, breathing, light, awakening...

Here are some phrases you might find useful as your meditate:

- I am at peace.

- I am peaceful.

- I embody peace.

- My heart is peaceful.

- I know peace.

- Peace is my truth.

- I am truthful.

- I embody truth.

- I am wise.

- I embody wisdom.

- I love wisdom.

- I embrace wisdom.

- I love to love.

- I love to be loved.

- I am love.

- I am loving.

- Love lives within me.

- I embody love.

- I choose love.

- I am kind.

- I am kindness.

- I embody kindness.

- I welcome kindness.

- I love kindness.

- Kindness dwells within.

- I forgive easily.

- I forgive wholeheartedly.

- I am open to forgiveness.

- I am open.

- I embody openness.

- My mind is open.

- My heart is open.

- My heart is kind.

- My mind is calm.

- I am calm.

- Calm envelops me.

- I breathe in calm energy.

- I welcome being calm.

- I am still.

- My mind is still.

- My thoughts are still.

- I embody stillness.

- I rejoice in stillness.

- I am wise.

- I possess great wisdom.

- Wisdom teaches me.

- Wisdom guides me.

- Wisdom is my friend.

- My mind is healthy.

- My body is healthy.

- I am healthy.

- I embody health.

- Health fills and surrounds me.

- I am whole.

- I am perfect and complete.

- Angels surround me.

- Angels guide me.

- Angels love me.

- Angels protect me.

- Angels heal me.

- Angels make me wise.

- Angels teach me to love.

- I am filled with grace.

- I choose grace.

- I express grace.

- I live in grace.

- I am truthful.

- I embody truth.

- I am one with truth.

- I am one with love.

- I am one with peace.

- I am one with kindness.

- I am one with gentleness.

- I am one with openness.

- I am one with integrity.

- I am one with God.

- I am one.

- I am.

- God is great.

- God is good.

- God is.

When you use a word, just state it once. Then relax, pause, and refocus your mind on your breathing. Try to hold and affirm the higher frequency in your mind. When you feel ready, move up to the next, higher frequency by stating a number that is one point or five, ten, or even twenty points higher. Let your intuition guide you. There is no right answer here. Again, if you need to move up very slowly, going point by point, then that's fine and right for you. If you're jumping forward quickly, that's fine too. Just don't rush it. It is far better to spend more time releasing the tension and discomfort that is often associated with the lower frequencies than it is to leap to the higher energy states while maintaining unresolved lower frequency energy blocks. Go slowly and take your time, returning often to do releasing work in the frequency ranges that feel uncomfortable to you.

# One Point Attention: Reaching 700

If Dr. Hawkins' scale describes the human energetic spectrum as encompassing a range from 0-1,000, why do I stop the guided meditations around frequency 710 or 730?

The frequency range from 700-710 (and in the low 700s in general) bathes you in an incredible sense of timeless well-being and peace. Problems don't exist. Not only has the monkey mind fallen completely silent, words have difficulty forming in the mind. Thinking continues, but it can be better described as awareness rather than as "thinking" with its typical connotations involving words and ideas moving through the mind.

At 710 and thereabouts, you're aware, you feel completely still, perfectly centered in your body and being, and utterly quiet. There is no laughter at this frequency, not because it's sad in any way but because it's just so quiet.

If you can enter the low 700s during meditation, you've mastered the art of meditation. When you reach this frequency range, all issues and concerns are resolved. What you might have thought of as problems before simply don't enter your mind at all. The pressing list of things that need doing no longer bothers you, no longer even occurs to you unless you purposely retrieve it.

You can still speak, but the speech is slow, gentle, and contains pauses. Words need some time to form in your mind. You can think about anything you like in this frequency range, but traditional thinking requires focus and conscious choice.

Whereas while you were in the lower frequencies, especially under frequency 500, you had to work hard to silence your thoughts, even briefly, at frequency 700 and above this pattern has now been reversed. Words and thoughts no longer occupy the space of your mind unless you willingly and willfully (the use of the will is very soft and subdued in this state) decide to bring them into your conscious mind for consideration. Otherwise, the silence reigns unchallenged.

You no longer grieve, worry, feel anger, or are afraid. All fears of aging, of financial insecurity, of being loved or not loved, of losing people you care about, and of death–all of these former preoccupations and fears resolve themselves completely, dissolving away into the deep stillness of presence.

Unfortunately, these cares, obligations, and preoccupations will return when you resume your normal day-to-day life below frequency 700. The difference now is that you have experienced the refined and holy state of 700 and above. You don't just know that it exists intellectually, you haven't just read about it or heard someone else recount his or her own experience, you have understood and seen it for yourself.

Your conscious mind can recall this peace, and during meditation you can practice returning to this gentle, rarified realm over and over. It is unlikely that problems will ever completely overwhelm your mind and life again. It is unlikely that your habituated emotional and thinking patterns will ever exert the same control over your being and your mind again. Even if they threaten to drown you in their familiar din and fears, there will be at least a little part of you that will remember your experience, even if it was brief, with Truth.

Starting at frequency 700, the past and the future are merely intellectual concepts that have resolved themselves into the fullness of this single moment, a singularity of still awareness that contains all of time within the focused presence of your being.

When you begin to visit the energetic range of the low 700s, you'll probably soon discover that you're in no hurry to leave this exalted state of being. You feel great. You feel more contentment and a greater sense of well-being than perhaps at any other time in your life.

Why would you want to leave?

It can be hard to leave the energetic spectrum of Frequency Meditation's ideal target goal of 700-730, and you may feel pulled to return to that frequency range often. You've been warned–we can want to retreat there as a form of escapism in an effort to get away from the pressures, demands, and angst of our ordinary lives. Certainly, spending a few minutes meditating at 700 or so, and it only takes a couple of minutes for the perfect calm and silence to settle all around you, is a far, far better choice for how to handle stress and painful emotions than yelling, doing drugs, drinking a lot of alcohol, expressing impatience or hostility toward the people around you, engaging in reckless behavior, and other kinds of unhealthy and low frequency behavior.

At the same time, we've come to this earth to have material, embodied lives. Our earthly lives provide us with countless opportunities through which to learn to deal with life's challenges and hardships. While focusing our attention on our physical bodies and lives, we get to practice remembering the deep spiritual truth of who we really are and where we really come from. We have the opportunity to connect to the elevated awareness resounding within despite being surrounded by voices and situations that would tempt us to forget our origin in love itself, our true home in the divine.

I believe that it is essential for our personal and spiritual growth to learn how to inhabit the high frequency range of energetic experience. At the same time, we need to then leave these high frequency states and return to our ordinary lives. We need to return to our normal daily functioning, ideally in the 310-520 range, while not dipping below 200 as much as we can possibly avoid it. We need to spend time with our family and friends. We need to go to work. We need to run errands, change the light bulbs, and clean the house. We need to return phone calls and answer email. There are a whole range of duties and mundane tasks that await us in the real world. Now, though, we can begin to perform them, say, at 350 while doing the yard work or at 370 while painting the house. We now can engage in these necessary and ordinary chores while maintaining a subtle connection to the higher frequencies, with a memory of God's perfect peace, with a greater presence and awareness.

I love the range of spiritual frequencies that begin in the 500s. They feel so positive, caring, supportive, and healing. I love to spend time in them during prayer and meditation. I move up into the 500-680 range to receive new insights, inspiration, and intuitive gifts of knowing and wisdom. I love it!

However, most of my daily life occurs primarily in the 350-520 range. Why? Because that is the range of highly effective functioning in the physical world. I don't want to drive my car in the 700s–that could be dangerous. The 350-520 range allows me to focus my mind on the things of the world, and it helps me to stay centered and grounded in my being and in my personal identity. At the same time, a little bit of my awareness can remain linked to the 500s and 600s when I'm at work or as I drive down the road so that I have a strong, intuitive connection to Spirit. I'm now driving with a heightened awareness of the other cars and of potential dangers, but my energy is centered, ideally, securely in the high 400s or low 500s.

With time and practice you can learn to safely drive and go about your daily business in the 500s range. It takes patience and some time. In order for daily life to be lived in a successful and healthy way from the perspective of the 500s, it is essential to have thoroughly cleared out the frequency range from 0-200. This clearing and releasing work could take months. It's more likely that in order to completely release it fully, it will take years. Once the lower frequency range has been fully cleared and you've learned how to live effectively and consistently from the 500s, you can gradually experiment with spending more of your daily life in the 600s. Take it slowly and please do not rush this process. The frequencies, beliefs, emotions, and habits under 200 are scary and uncomfortable, and it is easy to want to avoid or forget about them. However, until the frequency range from 0-200 has been utterly cleansed, forgiven, and released, we are not free or whole, and we cannot be wholly present and healthy as we walk through our lives. My books *Upgrade* and *The Alchemy of Change* (due to be published in 2015) both deal with ways in which to heal the lower frequency patterns in our lives and in our minds.

I believe that we have all entered this world to have a human experience, to learn about materiality, and to work with this physical dimension. This life is a huge gift, no matter how hard it can seem at times. Therefore, in order to fully embrace this gift of life, we honor it through service to other people and by going to work to contribute to the people around us, to the good, and to the realm of ideas and creativity in this world. We connect to the spiritual realms above 500, but we don't try to live most of our daily lives from that perspective. We have people with whom to share this journey, and our relationships will be limited and not fully engaged in in the human dimension if all we do with our friends and family is sit around silently in a state of calm bliss at 710.

Going to those high frequencies and bringing back the experience that we have there will help us be far kinder, gentler, wiser, and more generous human beings. I believe that we should travel to the high frequency dimensions and then return with insights gained and peace felt, sharing those experiences with the people in this world so in need of comfort, of peace, and of compassion.

# Labyrinth: The Frequency Range of the 800s

Once you've learned to spend some time in the 700s, whether on purpose or by accident, you might discover that you rise up higher still into the 800s during deep meditation.

Again, treat these high frequencies with respect. After hanging out in the 800s, you might not really want to return to the challenges and trials of your daily life. Excessive meditation can be a form of escapism, although it's a much healthier version of avoiding life, uncomfortable feelings, and difficult situations than those chosen by people who spend hours and hours watching TV on a regular basis, doing drugs, drinking too much, constantly playing computer or video games, gambling, getting engrossed in pornography, exercising compulsively, or otherwise fleeing being fully present and engaged in daily life.

The 800s, while also highly peaceful, silent, and calm, feel different than the 700s. In the 800s your body will begin to feel really weird, almost foreign, kind of heavy yet not dense at all. While firmly rooted to your chair and hyper-aware of your body, of its margins and form, you may have the sensation of floating, of tilting, or of rotating in space.

You may have an untethered feeling of intense being combined with a diminishing sense of yourself as a body.

Just as in the 700s the mind's chatter and thinking become still and words form only with some effort in your mind, and just as in the 700s you're aware of yourself as fully present in this one moment in time, which is time itself, in the 800s your concepts of space may begin to become unglued.

The 600s involve the final dissolution of the ego and the belief that you are somehow separate from other people. You'll have a reduced sense of yourself as a unique person with an identity that is separate from others. In the 600s you'll realize that you aren't "other" or different from your brothers on this earth.

The 700s involve the dissolution of the illusion of the flow of time. Time is released from the concept of something happening before and then zipping past this present moment on its hurried rush forward toward an imagined future.

The 800s involve the disruption of the concept of space. In the 800s, you're not really here or there because there isn't much of a here or there left. You begin to understand in a powerful way that your true existence occurs in this moment, in the only here and now that exists.

If you do find yourself floating about in the 800s, enjoy it briefly and then bring yourself back to the low 700s for the duration of your meditation practice by firmly stating "710" and then holding your consciousness there. When you're done meditating, bring your frequency back to under 500, do some grounding exercises to help you become fully present and centered, and then utter a quick prayer to ask what frequency you should occupy in order to perform, in the most helpful way, the tasks waiting patiently before you.

If the task awaiting you is making breakfast for your family and getting the kids off to school, inquire within what the perfect frequency would be for you to perform those tasks today. On a different day, the same tasks might prefer a different frequency based on a number of factors that the unconscious can take into account for you such as the weather, the moods of various family members, traffic that will be encountered, and so on. If you hear or sense the number "340," then internally affirm that you're now at that frequency, make sure that you're well-grounded and focused, and return to the people and tasks that surround you in your daily life.

Like the 700s, the 800s need to be treated with caution and great respect. Brief visits to the 800s in order to understand and experience that state are sufficient.

# Impermanence: Frequency 900

What's left to dissolve in the 900s? Our attachments to the earth and to this lifetime begin to release in the 900s. Our individual identity as a person with a name, gender, address, job, educational level, family, hobbies, opinions, likes and dislikes – all of these unravel very quickly in this range. They become little facts about the meditator who is sitting there; these little details hold only minimal interest to the eternal and perfect self that is shining forth into your consciousness the higher you move up into this range.

At the same time, the illusion of death fades in the 900s range. Death begins to be understood in a visceral rather than in an intellectual way, as a shift in energy state from one that is denser and slower-moving to one that is more refined, free, expansive, and joyful.

Unless you have reached the natural conclusion of your lifetime and are elderly indeed, I most strongly recommend that you try **not** to reach the 900s during meditation. If you do find yourself in the 900s, take a look around for a minute or two and then consciously and deliberately return yourself to frequency 710 for the rest of your meditation session. Then settle into the 490s when you're done meditating. Be sure to do some grounding exercises as well, as you always should after Frequency Meditation.

I recommend that you wait until you're nearing the natural conclusion of this lifetime before visiting or relaxing into the 900s frequency range. The 900s prepare you to complete your lifetime in a joyous and blessed way. In the 900s the fear of death is not possible because it is seen merely as a stepping stone out of your human body and into the next phase of your adventures in consciousness and ever-expanding awareness. I believe that when someone who is very elderly or ill nears the end of his or her lifetime and begins to speak with relatives and other loved ones on "the other side," he or she is probably spending some time in the 900s frequency range.

When he or she starts to "hallucinate" and talk about events and experiences from other times and places or ones that do not make sense to their family and caretakers, or when he or she is slipping in and out of a coma or has lapsed into a coma, that person is now preparing to leave his or her body by spending time in the 900s range. In the 900s the wisdom, the voices, and the call of the ranges and stages beyond frequency 1,000 can communicate with us and help us transition out of one state of being and into the next.

When the time is right, you'll simply release your body and enter the realms above and beyond the human maximum of frequency 1,000 as you approach the bright white light of God.

# Mandalas: Frequency Meditation – A Transformative Practice

The secret to effective Frequency Meditation is to consciously and successively tune into the various frequencies in the body and in your personal energy field. Each point along our human energy range contains information. As we tune into a particular frequency of energy, we access the information held, in our bodies, minds, and in the energetic or auric field that surrounds us, at that frequency point.

By practicing Frequency Meditation, meditators are consciously and actively clearing emotional blockages, difficult memories and experiences, and even physical complaints from the physical, emotional, mental, and other energetic aspects of their being.

This healing and clearing work is effective, comparatively easy and painless, and provides long-term, lasting results. At the same time, it requires patience, perseverance, and diligence.

Over time, practitioners of Frequency Meditation naturally resonate at a higher frequency, their thinking is clearer and more focused, they experience greater ease concentrating and staying on task, and their relationships, work, and health begin to function more smoothly and happily.

Frequency Meditation deepens and improves one's experiences while meditating. More importantly, it can help to release emotional disturbances and erratic thinking, depression, grief, anger, guilt, and other energetic blockages that may have impeded contented, peaceful, and effective living.

Frequency Meditation, when practiced with gentleness, consistency, and care, helps its practitioners live life more happily and successfully.

# Mantras: Conclusion

It is my hope that this book introduced you, easily and with clarity, to a new form of meditation practice that combines different methods of energy work together with my own spiritual insights and received guidance. Frequency Meditation is designed to help everyone develop their meditation skills, from those new to meditation and just getting started to advanced practitioners of meditation. Not content to simply calm the body-mind, Frequency Meditation guides its practitioners to high-level energetic states of perfect silence and stillness.

In this book I didn't include a description of the many and diverse benefits of meditation because they're so well-known to most people interested in meditation and because detailed descriptions of the medical and psychological gains that meditating regularly will provide for you can be easily accessed in a range of books on the subject and on the Internet.

I hope that this book was easy to read and follow and provided you with a variety of helpful suggestions and techniques to enable you to successfully start to meditate or to improve your ongoing meditation discipline. I hope that it inspired you to deepen your spiritual practice and to meditate on a regular basis.

Peace to your heart.

# The Lake of Peace:

# Recommended Readings

Brach, Tara, Ph.D. *True Refuge: Finding Peace and Freedom in Your Own Awakened Heart.* Bantam Books, NY. 2013.

Brach's book speaks powerfully from the first person, describing some of her experiences as a teacher and counselor who uses meditation, and the insights to be gained from its practice, as a primary tool with clients. Her book is candid, clear, and full of helpful suggestions and meaningful stories. *True Refuge* is an engaging read that will inspire the reader to meditate.

Hawkins, David, M.D., Ph.D. *Healing and Recovery.* Veritas Publishing, Sedona, AZ. 2009.

Reading Hawkins' book, *Healing and Recovery*, I realized that we're all in recovery from something. This book contains Hawkins' clearest explanation of his energy frequency scale and helps the reader understand what to expect at the key stages of that scale. The book is repetitive, but in a mostly helpful way, reiterating key concepts so that the reader may gradually bypass the resistance of habitual belief characteristic of the logical mind.

Hawkins, David, M.D., Ph.D. *Power vs. Force: The Hidden Determinants of Human Behavior.* The Author's Official Authoritative Edition. Hay House, Inc., Carlsbad, CA. 2013.

I recommend the book, *Power vs. Force*, to people more than any other work. Although not always easy to follow, this volume provides a thorough explanation of the importance of muscle testing and of how to use it in conjunction with Hawkins' frequency scale. Hawkins discusses various findings from his years of research using the scale he developed. This is an informative and potentially life-changing book, but densely written and a fairly difficult read.

LeShan, Lawrence, *How to Meditate: A Guide to Self-discovery.* Little, Brown and Company, Boston, MA. 1999.

*How to Meditate* is the first book I ever read, in its original 1975 edition, about how to meditate. LeShan wrote a clear, direct, and helpful guide for those interested in learning to meditate or for anyone interesting in discovering more about a range of meditative practices. This book is a classic in the field and continues to guide students of meditation on ways to expand and deepen their practice. In his 90s at the time of this writing, LeShan has clearly gained enormous personal benefit from his years spent meditating and teaching others to do so.

Nahmad, Claire. *The Book of Peace: Meditations from Around the World*. Journey Editions, Boston, MA. 2003.

*The Book of Peace* is a lovely volume that explains meditation practices from different countries. Written in blues, white, and greens, even its design and layout help to calm the mind. This book contains useful little charts and inspiring images on which to focus in contemplative silence. Nahmad also includes a number of affirmations, scattered throughout the text, for readers to use as they work to become more aware and present in their lives. The author discusses meditation in terms of the chakras and focuses on how meditation can be used to cultivate peace in oneself and in the world.

Singer, Michael A. *The Untethered Soul: The Journey Beyond Yourself*. New Harbinger Publications, Inc., Oakland, CA. 2007.

I loved this book, especially the part about imagining the inner, constant mind noise as an unpleasant roommate. Singer talks about the different "selves" that make up our sense of who we are. The author challenges the reader to go deeper and to connect to the witnessing presence at the root of our being. *The Untethered Soul* is an insightful and engaging read about the difficulties encountered by meditators and the wisdom that may be gained from a meditation practice.

Tolle, Eckhart. *The Power of Now: A Guide to Spiritual Enlightenment.* New World Library, Novato, CA. 1999.

In *The Power of Now*, Tolle invites the reader to become more conscious, aware, and centered in the moment. This book is designed to be read slowly so that one has time to try out the exercises presented and to allow the ideas discussed to gently percolate into one's consciousness. This is an excellent book full of wisdom and helpful suggestions for those interested in meditation and in becoming more conscious in their daily lives.

The author:

Ellen Hartsfield recently left a university teaching career to focus instead on finishing and publishing the many books she is working on. In addition, she is developing a specialized coaching practice centered on intuitive guidance received in high frequency meditative states. Over the years she has acquired the full spectrum of intuitive abilities, from clairvoyance and clairaudience to the other subtle vehicles that "psychic" information can take, including dreams and clairsentience.

Each guidance session is given over to Spirit to help clients gently release old wounds without needing to analyze, re-experience, or interpret them. Clients are supported in developing a personal connection to their own internal teacher, to the source of wisdom that resides within their being.

Ellen has discovered that everyone's intuitive faculties develop as they clear their lower energetic frequencies, such as those energy blockages around the energetic states of fear and anger, and as they learn to inhabit the higher frequencies (410 and higher) on a consistent basis. She uses her intuition and insights to support the clearing of energetic blockages in the clients' systems, helping them leave the lower energetic states behind them and move into the more joyful, peaceful, and easy life flow provided by the higher frequency range.

Ellen has studied a number of different energy healing traditions and has read countless books on the subject. She has also been a student of *A Course in Miracles* for nearly three decades. Ellen has discovered that her best and most rapid learning now occurs when she centers herself within a high frequency intuitive state (550-750) and listens deeply.

Made in the USA
Middletown, DE
13 May 2021